Bacchus And The Drinker

Also by Jim Levy

Nonfiction
    Corazón (and Merkle)

Poetry
    Cooler Than October Sunlight
    The Poems of Caius Herennius Felix
    Monet's Eyes
    Seen From A Distance

Essays
    Joy to Come
    Chekhov's Mistress

Memoirs
    The Fifth Season
    Rowdy's Boy
    Those Were the Days (with Phaedra Greenwood)

Travel and Fiction
    Mar Egeo

Bacchus And The Drinker

New and Selected Poems Inspired By Art

Jim Levy

Atalaya Press

Copyright © 2021 by Jim Levy

All rights reserved. No part of this publication may be reproduced, distributed, or transmitted in any form or by any means, including photocopying, recording, or other electronic or mechanical methods, without the prior written permission of the authors, except in the case of brief quotations embodied in critical reviews and certain other noncommercial uses permitted by copyright law.

Atalaya Press

Printed in the United States of America

ISBN: 978-1-7337940-6-0

To all artists, those who seek, those who find, those who sit in the weeds without hope,

and to Phaedra, Sara and Alexander, whose love and life have sustained me.

Contents

Author's Note xi
Note On The Text xiii

The Voyage, Initially Toward Love

Hölderlin In Arroyo Hondo 1
Arrows Lose Their Lift 4
The Infinite 6
By The Third Glass 7
Reading In The Sun 9
Under The Stars 12
From Debauchery Comes Beauty 14
At Eight Bells (Noon) Exactly 18
The Map And The Cage 22
Rhetoric 25
I Left The House One Day 31
Seeing The World 33
The Clack Of The Dice 34
Canto Hondo 37
Where The Piñon Jays Gather 43
Neither Of Us Running 45
Snakes Shed Their Skin 46
Best Poem Ever 48

How Miraculous The Music

From The Daily Courant 53
Listening To Dvořák's 56
I Can Taste It 57
The Dance 59
I Wake To Waves And Voices 61
Errico Beyle, Milanese 62
The Raga 64
Cante Jondo 66
Risking Tickets 69
Different Drum 72
Nights In White Satin 75
The 17th Day, Partway 76
MP3 On A Summer Day 78
He's In The Back Booth 80

The Proper Distance

The Proper Distance 85
What Is The Proper Distance? 88
Susanna And The Elders 89
Zeus, Besotted With Her Beauty 92
Two Bacchae 93
They're Very Different, These Three Nudes 95
Only Air Beneath Me 97
Le Suicidé 99

The Light At Daybreak 101

The Photographer 106

The Idiot-Savant Says 108

Easter 110

THE DAY DAWNED BRIGHT

Death Of Gilgamesh 115

Hot Day In August 117

Daphne Slowed By Mud 119

The Music Wakes The Foxes 121

Frieze Of Girls With Lovely Braids 123

The Other One 125

Theseus In The Maze 126

Ariadne's Llament 128

In The Great Hall 130

Astarte In Hades 131

Priapus's Complaint 132

THE HOUR IS GETTING LATE

Branch Bent Down With Snow 137

And I Said, Oh Place 141

Rilke In Ronda 142

Me Gusta la Vida Enormemente 146

Comprenderán Todos Los Hombres 148

Maktub 150

Even When It's Dark 154

Drape The Day In Precious Linen 159
What Of The Night 161
She Must Have Been Large 164
They'll Meet In Heaven, Stars 166
Death In Venice (Calif) 169
Isle Full Of Sweet Airs 171
A Word Then 172
The Poet 175
Like A Jeweler 176
Best Poem Ever 2 178

Author's Note

The composer Lukas Foss said in an interview that all art, even the most original, is influenced by the art that preceded it. He compared artists to the anonymous stone masons who built the European cathedrals, all working on one vast edifice called Art.

And why not? Artists draw inspiration from nature, love, death and, more than is usually acknowledged, from the art they experience. There is an uneven but discernable line from Gilgamesh and the Bible to Milton and Yeats; from Greek dance and Medieval plays to Fellini and Spielberg; from cave paintings and Roman frescos to Poussin and Monet, each building on and adding to the body of what we call Western civilization. The poet Kathleen Raine wrote, "A culture is precisely this inheritance, of a language and a literature, a *corpus* of music, painting, and all the arts."

I am 80, with poor hearing and worse eyesight, and having mined my youth and middle age and even to some extent my old age, I have written a book of poems that are in response to some work of art, whether it be another poem, a painting, a piece of music, or a myth. After each poem, I have added some notes on the artist or the art that inspired me. This is my way of adding some small portion to the collaboration we call art."

Jim Levy
March 2021
Arroyo Hondo, New Mexico

Note On The Text

Most of my poems are original but some, following Pound and Lowell, are rough adaptations of poems by others. Still others are "in the manner of" Hölderlin, Vallejo, Bishop, Rilke and Mandelstam. Some use the lyrics of pop music, just as Li Po and Tu Fu mined the music of the taverns of their day.

Translations, whether rough or close, free or faithful, are mine. If the original poem is in Italian, Spanish, Portuguese or French, I have used the original as well as English translations as guides. For Chinese, Greek and Russian, I have relied on the translations of others.

To quote Vasily Zhukovsky, Russian translator of Homer, Virgil, Goethe, and Byron, "Almost everything of mine is someone else's or about someone else, and yet it is all my very own."

I am particularly indebted to the accurate and poetic translations by A. S. Kline which can be found on his fascinating web site, Poetry In Translation.

Picasso famously said, "good artists borrow, great artists steal." All artists do both. Pound lifted poems from Li Po, Shostakovich used chords and motifs from Prokofiev, Mandelstam incorporated lines from Homer, Villon, Baudelaire. So I have borrowed and stolen, adapted and imitated, distorted and mangled – call it pastiche, montage, echo, homage, or plagiarism, there is all of that.

In the movie Il *Postino,* the postman copied poems by Neruda and, claiming to having written them, sends them to his lover. Caught, he says, "Poetry doesn't belong to those who write it. It belongs to those who need it."

The Voyage, Initially Toward Love

Hölderlin In Arroyo Hondo

The Atalaya ridge runs behind the house.
To the south, the Llano ridge.
Between them, the little Rio Hondo
that once glittered with gold.
Snakes are dreaming in the ravines,
blackbirds are mobbing a hawk
and deer descend with their young
to boldly graze on winter wheat.
Snow drenches the fields framed
by black poplars. In May wild roses
line the banks of the ditches
and the valley floor flowers.
But it is the poverty, the poverty
of this valley mired in time,
that for me from the start has been its beauty.

It is sweet sleeping with the window open
hearing in my dream the sound of the little river,
and sweet, sitting above the river with a notebook
writing poems that say what I see and how I feel.
Walking by the river on the path
through the dry cottonwood leaves
past the plum hedges and blackberry thickets,
I talk with the water wondering what the water knows.
This, the little river and its voices,
matters to me more than the rest,
but in the middle of our discourse,
a raven arrives with news of heaven:
the vanishing world is everywhere.

I would awake the rude adobes
with their mud floors hardened with ox blood,
walk the white dusty road through the village,
both the upper and lower village,
unseal the wells in the courtyards
and the pit houses for potatoes and onions.
I would restore the squat stone watchtowers
at both ends of the valley,
to watch for invaders and shout the alarm
that sounds like Atalaya.

Apples, ripe, plunged into fire,
a comet bursting into flame,
grasses along the ditches burning in spring,
the red day dying in a pond.
Thus they depart the world.
I die differently, curled inward,
in the darkest shadows.
My heart made of crystal
longs for dissolution.
The river runs under the ice
sounding like cold water poured into silver cups.

Falling asleep in the orchard to the sound of insects,
in the forest under a pine tree
to the sound of wind in the treetops,
at the river, burrowing into the sand for warmth –
sleep is my brother, a rival, or sister, tender.
Falling asleep in the womb the first, the only, paradise.

Hölderlin in Arroyo Hondo

Friedrich Hölderlin, German poet, was born in 1770 and lived as a tutor and poet until he went mad at age thirty-seven. He was placed into the care of a sympathetic cabinet maker and lived for the next thirty-six years in a small tower overlooking the river Neckar. His poems, hymns and fragments expressed his love of nature, celebrated ancient Greece, and pondered life and death.

> Ripe, plunged into fire, the fruit
> is tested on this earth
> and it is law, that all things pass
> like snakes dreaming on the hills of heaven.
> There is much to bear
> and all paths seem evil.
> Ancient laws of earth go astray like horses
> and we long for dissolution.
> But loyalty's a must!
> We should not look forward or back
> but learn to be rocked serenely,
> a small boat on the sea.
> Hölderlin

Arrows Lose Their Lift

Wilhelm Waiblinger, starting at age seventeen, visited Hölderlin off and on for four years.

A gaunt figure in the center of a circular room,
a gaze that has lost its fire.
He bows deeply, says "Hello Your Holiness"
and speaking to himself about himself,
he talks but in what language?
He says it is the Kalamatta tongue.
His face spasms, hands convulse,
his contortions mirror what's left of mind.
Immersed in rage and reverie,
he flies in an eccentric orbit around what is.

Another visit, in the summer.
"Come Friedrich, let's take a walk."
"Oh I can't Your Majesty, I don't have time."
"Come, we'll be back in time," a pun that's lost
on this lost soul. And off we go, hands in pocket
in the heat of day, to where fresh water gulls
float above the Neckar and honey bees,
sacred to Persephone, assail the pastures.
"Oh Holy Father, I once sang the virtues of this valley."

In the winter, fields cracked with cold
and wasps falling to the ground like apples,
we stayed indoors and sang.
He played the piano, a simple theme
over and over. I gave him tobacco
and he gave me little poems,
flickers of his genius.

"Remote in April, remote in June,
I pay in grief for thought and art."
Asking questions, he responds himself,
sometimes yes, sometimes no. He adores the no's.
He says, "observe, kind sir, I have a sofa now."
"Love," he says, "is lost but loyalty, it is a must."

Hölderlin knows that the bright streak
on the river leads to second childhood.
He knows the meaning of the phosphorescence
in the rotting wood. There's only half-life
in the shadow of the bell.
Did losing Father drive him mad?
Did loving Mother cause his self's undoing?
Unable to gain a purchase on a thing or thought,
madness is his art, and like art
it draws on innerness and life's dark matter.

He thought that what he wanted
would transpire but arrows lose their lift
when the sun comes near.
Before the rain, the angry thunder's
speaking to the lightning.
The suffering god who loves us is disloyal.
A nameless planet gleams at dusk.
The stars recede like starlings with screams of joy.

Arrows Lose Their Lift

Waiblinger wrote an essay about his visits with Hölderlin called *Life, Poetry and Madness*. A minor poet, he died in Rome at the age of twenty-five and was buried in the Protestant Cemetery along with Keats and Shelley.

The Infinite

Sitting on the hill of rock and cactus,
sitting and gazing at the village below,
trailers and old adobes and snow-streaked fields,
and beyond, a pale moon over small extinct volcanos
and beyond those, an expanse of nothing,
I am reminded of Leopardi's poem
when he too sat above his town
looking out beyond the hedges
to the infinity of space and said
that it was sweet to wreck in such a sea.

The Infinite

> I've always loved this solitary hill
> sitting and gazing out at endless space,
> listening to the monstrous silence.
> When wind rustles through the tops of trees
> I compare that sound to silence.
> When I feel all the dead seasons
> and the immensity of the present,
> it is sweet to shipwreck in this sea.
>   Leopardi

By The Third Glass

If I could resurrect one writer to be with this afternoon
with this bottle of wine,
it wouldn't be Lowry,
he would drink the bottle in a flash and disappear,
or Lawrence who would lecture me,
or Kerouac, a silly man.
Perhaps da Cunha, a solid engineer
or Martin du Gard, who has a capacity for friendship
or better, someone who is now obscure,
but not Pessoa, he's too shy
and there's too many of him.

Forget it. Call my dog. She is lying in the warmth
left in the grass, the creature who understands me best.

No Germans need apply
or Swiss or Scandinavians,
Russians are too emotional,
Li Po talks too much,
Plath is obsessing about Hughes
and Hughes is obsessing about some other woman.
Mudd is not dead yet.
None of the drunks – there are so many –
none of the academics for obvious reasons.
Stendhal is a possibility,
we could talk Napoleon, Milan and opera buffa,
or Marquez, but he just died and may still smell.
Lorca, Proust, I doubt they would find me attractive.

You know where this is going.
A sad and solitary man
who loved a teenage girl who died.
He taught, wrote a few poems,
fled Franco to France and died there
of a broken life.
I imagine a medium priced white from Soria
and we talk but by the third glass,
he cuts the thread between us
and disappears into a private solitude,
as I do, unable to share our sorrows
which delight us.

By The Third Glass

A sad and solitary man. Antonio Machado, Spanish poet born in Sevilla in 1875, who, despite my poem, wasn't much of a drinker.

> One summer evening
> my balcony and door
> were open to the air
>
> What death tore
> was a thread between us.
> Machado

Reading In The Sun

They said it already,
in Marlowe-speak and Yeats'
voice seeping into mine
and mine unmanned and old
ashamed that I have placed
my trust in old books and oblivion.
And then Machado's voice
that says Soria is air
Soria is sorrow
and I write my Solitudes.

Reading In The Sun

John Dos Passos spent an evening with Machado in Segovia, sitting in a casino watching a game of billiards and talking about Whitman and Dickinson, then strolling around the city with a couple of other men. Decades later, he remembered Machado as "a large sad fumbling man dressed like an old-fashioned schoolteacher. Stiff wing collar none too clean; spots on his clothes . . . always when I think of him he is wearing the dusty derby he wore the evening we walked around Segovia in the moonlight."

Juan Ramón Jiménez wrote that Machado was "corpulent, a naturally earthy bulk, like a big stump just dug out of the ground; he dressed his oversized body in loose-fitting black, ocher or brown clothes, in keeping with his extravagant manner of living death; a new jacket perhaps, hurriedly bought in the outdoor market, baggy trousers, and a completely frayed all-season overcoat which was not the proper size; he wore a hat with sagging threadbare brim."

There is something silly or outrageous about such a large shabby man going about with an air of melancholy. Hamlet was thin, and Don Quixote too. One wonders if Dos Passos and Jiménez didn't inadvertently reveal the comic side of Machado's person.

Under the scruffy exterior lay a complex man. Dario wrote, "he was luminous and deep/ as a man of good faith" (which is to say, authentic, the opposite of the existentialists' man of bad faith). And Dos Passos continued: "A lonely widower, in his forties, he gave the impression of being helpless in life's contests and struggles, a man without defenses... Long ago he had accepted the pain and ignominy of being what he was, a poet, a man who had given up all hope of reward to live for the delicately imagined mood, the counterpoint of words, the accurately recorded ear. Machado el Bueno, his friends called him... He followed his calling with the simplicity and abnegation of a monk. Early he must have vowed himself to poverty."

Looking deeper, Jimenez wrote, "Even as a child, Antonio Machado sought death, the dead, and decay in every recess of his soul and body. He always held within himself as much of death as of life, halves fused together in ingenious artistry. A poet of death, Machado spent hour after hour meditating upon, perceiving, and preparing for death; I have never known anyone else who so balanced these levels [of life and death] and who by his living-dying overcame the gap between these existences, paradoxically opposed yet the only ones known to us."

Under The Stars

It was spring and I was sitting as usual
under the flowering plum
and raised my glass to the moon
and said have a drink.
You know how sober the moon is.
So I looked down at my shadow
the one that faithfully follows me around
and said, you, drink up
and it did
and the moon, left out, decided to have one too
and soon we're singing,
the moon warbling along and I was dancing
and my shadow was wobbling like a drunk
and the three of us were friends forever
but after more drinks
we wandered off in different directions.
Join us and we'll do it again, the four of us,
under the stars.
     from a poem by Li Po

Under The Stars

Although Li Po (usually spelled Li Bai now) mentions drinking with friends, I think he was a solitary drunk, but it is difficult to say anything definitive about him. Like most artists, there were at least three of him, the actual Li Po, the self-created Li Po, and the Li Po of biographers, admirers and moralists.

 So many names: Li Po, Li Bai, Li Bo, Li T'ai Po, Li Twelve by his family and friends because he was twelfth among his brothers and cousins.

 Like the desert sands from which he came, he was shifty,

rootless, a *Xian,* happy, carefree, powerful.

A brilliant swordsman "who killed many." And a consummate tourist, visiting tombs, temples, shrines, mountains and lakes wherever he traveled.

Tall, straight, with excellent bone structure, he wore the black embroidered hat of a Daoist but birds didn't land on him when he called them and he nearly overdosed on "longevity pills."

Spare me, he wasn't a fish named Kun a hundred miles long. He called himself "the great *roc*" but he wasn't spiritually free.

He had ambitions for a prestigious government post but he insulted or humiliated his bosses and got nowhere. Easily duped, he was something of a child in the world.

He drank "300 cups of wine" at a go. A good companion the way some drunks are, and a good friend, but a terrible husband and, although sentimental, a terrible father.

He wrote movingly about lotus flowers rising from limpid waters, meaning barmaids and escorts.

He drowned, as everyone knows, when he drunkenly dove overboard trying to embrace the reflection of the moon.

Or, as others suppose, of chronic lung disease, pus penetrating his lungs, brought on by his alcoholism.

Either way, he rode away on the back of a whale toward the moon, his heaven an extension of life on earth but with better flora, loving pets, and better wine.

He was *Jiuxian,* Wine Immortal, and at death, *Zhexian,* Banished Immortal because of his behavior, and now he is *Shixian,* Poet Immortal.

In other words, a great poet. I have to take their word for it. All those characters running top to bottom right to left.

From Debauchery Comes Beauty
for Constantine Cavafy

I never loved just the poems.
I loved the man too,
the one who watched the world through glasses
that magnified his memories.
The glasses are the clue,
round as circles which framed
his soft gray opal eyes that swam like fish
up to the glass and peered out at the shabby streets
and shabby creatures of the city that he loved
and longed to leave. More Greek than Arab,
misty in the mornings, sun-drenched,
marginal in every way: Alexandria.

He worked mornings cloaked in anonymity
writing letters, checking figures,
estimating costs, for little pay
and an elusive satisfaction.
He came alive at night in the district
near the Custom's House
sitting in a back room of a tavern
half-hidden by a curtain
fondling a young man,
a clerk or hustler, a beautiful boy
from the blacksmith's or a dry goods store,
one of those who came from Greece
to work long hours for a few piasters.

Then to Attarine, the sordid district
where he kept a room to lie

with young men clothed in flesh
and enjoy a pagan love of limbs,
the act itself instantly dissolved
in moonlight and in memory.

Weekends, holidays, some evenings
his art emerged from vain remorse
that never lasted long. He found time
for poems in which he mixed plain speech
with mandarin, a dialectic like his life,
drab hours in the office followed by
lush hours of imagination.
He moved from the back streets
of Attarine to the ancient world
which over time became a seamless blend
of elegance and ironies. He confused
his memories of young men
with sensual, sometimes cynical
young men from Roman outposts.
Did emotion cloud his memory?
How much of it was real?
How many of his lovers lived
only in his mind? It doesn't matter.
From debauchery came beauty.

When old he frizzed his hair
and dyed it to deflect the blows of aging.
Although desire dropped away and became
loose sheets of paper, it existed
in the cherished object, love's body as a poem.

From Debauchery Comes Beauty

Constantine Cavafy, born in 1863, worked in the Third Circle of Irrigation at the Ministry of Public Works in Alexandria for three years as an unpaid clerk, hoping for a permanent position, and when he got it, stayed for thirty years as a valued member of the agency. Beyond the modest salary, he appreciated his job because the office closed at noon.

He wrote 154 poems, left 77 unpublished and repudiated 27. He preferred to publish in small, local magazines or in self-printed chap books that he shared with anyone interested. Of the poems he did publish, as soon as they were sent to the printer, he had regrets, a new idea, a phrase. He questioned the poems' right to exist.

His most important poems were written after his fortieth birthday and published two years after his death. They are often set in marginal Hellenic places during obscure historic times. He himself was marginal, rarely participating in the literary or political life of Egypt or Greece.

> I loiter in the taverns and brothels of Beirut.
> I didn't want to stay in Alexandria
> because Tamides left me –
> he went off with the Governor's son
> and got himself a villa on the Nile.
> I felt horrible, staying after that
> so I wallow with the lowlife of Beirut.
> It's a sordid life, and the one thing
> that saves me, like deathless beauty,
> like perfume that clings to my flesh,
> is that Tamides, the most beautiful of young men,
> was mine for two years

and not for a villa on the Nile either.
                                    Cavafy

I sit in a mood of reverie musing
about how I brought to art desires
and sensations, things half glimpsed:
faces, limbs, indistinct memories
of unfulfilled loves.

Let us submit to the art
that knows how to shape beauty,
blending impressions, connecting days to days,
almost imperceptibly completing life.
                                    from Cavafy

At Eight Bells (Noon) Exactly

    I will not sing
    Of my too loving mother and a distant father,
    a pair in love, for it was love at first
    and only later ugly. The long lugubrious days
    in Cleveland listening to the squabbling
    of the landlocked Candy Magnate and his Grace
    did not make me. God made me and remade me
    as I am and will be, here, forever
    at the bottom of the sea.

It was in fact his parents' bickering
that maddened him and worse, it was their cooing
followed by their short and nasty make-up sex
that drove him, age fifteen, to the first slight slash of wrist
that no one noticed; then he swallowed mother's Veronal
washed down with rum. He walked the island
through the orange groves singing in the moonlight,
and the sound of surf became his meter
and what he saw his images, slabs of marble
that did not weep, tarantulas that crawled
the sandy graves of perished sailors,
giant turtles spiked, flipped over and eviscerated.
Carib weather coiled, cracked
and struck the island with intent.

His voyage, initially toward love,
crossed new thresholds, turned toward the shadows.
Red hair graying early, a wasted face,
a naked sensibility happiest when drowning
in the drink of bathtub gin and seeking love

from Polish and Puerto Rican seaman
in dockside alleys and the urinals of parks.

Because the vortex of his life was downward
he wrote inward, broken poems
fueled by alcohol and founded on false myths
of an America that never was
to proclaim a vision of it that will never be.
He riddled them with tortured syntax, tangled tropes
and clotted words, learning early that trafficking
in rhetoric was one way to belie his penury
and conceal his inclinations. Still, his complex art
lives in us who came to it in youth
and try in vain to write the same bold music.
Among the wreckage, some lines live,
regulated by the moon in metered truth
and by the logic of his metaphors.
They couple sound and sense and raise invention
to illumination. Just how many, five, fifteen,
maybe fifty lines survive and were they worth
a life of torment? Yes. His brittle fame,
bleached by time, meets the test of genius.

Although sweet Emil told him sailors rarely learn to swim
for swimming just delays the drowning
and warned him love at sea is not entirely amorous,
he went below the night before
to feel the fright of smoky sailor-sex,
was robbed of ring and wallet
and was beaten senseless and discarded.
One witness said, at eight bells (noon) exactly,
after waking without words and drinking breakfast

from a bottle, still in his pajamas,
he hung his topcoat neatly on the rail,
rose on tiptoe like a dancer, returned to earth,
then vaulted over and was gone.
He discovered that beyond our earthly shores
a third world, harsh, of water, tests the word,
and consigns us to a cruel oblivion
at the bottom of the sea.

At Eight Bells (Noon) Exactly

In the first stanza of my poem I assume the voice of Hart Crane, American poet. It references his father, who owned candy factories, and his mother Grace. In the next stanza, Veronal was the brand name for a barbiturate; Crane swallowed eighteen packets of it at age fifteen.

The island is the Isle of Pines, an island thirty-one miles south of Cuba where Crane's mother owned a plantation that no longer produced any fruit. He spent several months there as a teen, and again ten years later when he wrote much of his greatest poetry. He witnessed the hurricane that hit the island in October, 1926.

among the urinals. "Love," Crane wrote in *The Bridge*, is "a burnt match skating in a urinal." He was a sex addict who frequented waterfronts and parks wherever he was. When prowling, he sometimes used the name Mike Drayton, after the Elizabethan dramatist.

tortured syntax. Although Crane's poetry is dense and sometimes incomprehensible, it is built on a bedrock of blank verse which at times achieves a complexity and beauty equal to the Elizabethans.

he went below the night before. Strangely, Crane sailed on the ship S.S. Orazaba three times, from New York to Cuba in 1926, New York to Vera Cruz in 1931, and the final time a year later, from Vera Cruz destined for New York. About 275 miles north of Havana, he leapt overboard on April 27, 1932, age thirty-two. Due to alcoholism he had run out of poetry. In desperation, he had become engaged to an old friend, Peggy Cowley, who was on board, but he knew he could not be suitably married to a woman. The engines of the Orazaba were two steam turbines each with two screws, and although a passenger said she saw Crane swimming, it is likely that the screws churned him up immediately. The captain turned the ship around and sent lifeboats but the body wasn't found.

>   Above the fresh ruffles of the surf
>   Bright striped urchins flay each other with sand.
>   They have contrived a conquest for shell shucks,
>   And their fingers crumble fragments of baked weed
>   Gaily digging and scattering.
>
>   And in answer to their treble interjections
>   The sun beats lightning on the waves,
>   The waves fold thunder on the sand;
>   And could they hear me I would tell them:
>
>   O brilliant kids, frisk with your dog,
>   Fondle your shells and sticks, bleached
>   By time and the elements; but there is a line
>   You must not cross nor ever trust beyond it
>   Spry cordage of your bodies to caresses
>   Too lichen-faithful from too wide a breast.
>   The bottom of the sea is cruel.
>   Hart Crane

The Map And The Cage
for Elizabeth Bishop

You sought a room, a wicker chair,
a wooden table painted blue
or yellow, a shelf of books, Herbert, Hopkins,
Boehme, and Gibbons on decline and fall
where you wrote of Crusoe's island
and Calypso's cave, polished poems
that would define you
and settle something finally.
Some called it prison or a cage
but for you, a room was like a bower
where you could fashion feelings
into language and grow flowers
in a jar and deny that dying
is the writing on the wall.

Your poems are founded on capacity
for fact and observation. The first act
is to watch the world and see exactly.
You take objects for your subjects –
a beast, a plant, a birdcage or a map
that gives you access to your inner life.
You love maps.
It is nice to know that west is left
and north is at the top,
good to know where water ends and land begins.
Each name, like feeling, flows across
the place it names in tiny script.
Although seeing maps is healing,
mishaps happen, inlets get misplaced,

entire countries warped to fit the scale,
the world collapsed into a likeness.
Names overlap, boundaries blur,
colors that were delicate
fall from grace and fade.
You discovered, naming is not having,
having is not loving.

You wrote about your flights
to Paris, Italy, Brazil, places that came
with wealthy lovers.
Everywhere you drank, and stopped,
a constant round of booze and Antabuse,
like your peers, Thomas, Berryman and Lowell,
so compelling in the men, so mortifying in a woman.
Yeats said perfection of the life or of the work.
You opted for your art to say the least,
your life a mess, with complicated loves
and bourbon by the quart.

Lowell, friend and rival,
wrote of loves and rages,
airing out his grievances in print.
You said, art ain't worth that much.
Better to lock those things in cages
than let them breathe the air.

The trotting of your meter, dum da dum,
that he objected to and envied,
a sonnet with its subtle rhymes,
a sestina made of coffee, crumbs and sun
and sun and crumbs and coffee,
and a villanelle, about the art of losing:

you wrote it isn't hard to master
and then went on to rhyme it with disaster,
faster, vaster, five tight tercets
followed by a quatrain,
poems like woodwork jig-sawed into pieces
that fit perfectly, old lumber
that will weather time and last.

Poems must never scream the way
your mother screamed in the asylum.
So you wrote your poems
that have been labelled cool
and perfect. As with your shyness
and your gauche behavior,
they held hidden meanings
within their rules and strategies,
like mists to walk through into sudden sunlight.

The Map And The Cage

Poems must never scream. When Elizabeth Bishop was five, her mother was committed to an asylum in Dartmouth, Nova Scotia, where she died eighteen years later, age fifty-four.

> Mapped waters are more quiet than the land is,
> lending the land their waves' own conformation:
> and Norway's hare runs south in agitation,
> profiles investigate the sea, where land is.
> Are they assigned, or can the countries pick their colors?
> – what suits the character or the native waters best.
> Topography displays no favorites; North's as near as West.
> More delicate than the historians' are the map-makers' colors.
>
> Bishop

Rhetoric

Being something of a voyeur myself
I loved your poem, its rhymes and rhythms
and the blue-shadowed silk
worn by Susanna in the green water
– but I was young.
Now I wonder at the rhetoric and the range
of devices that ornament the poem.
Why not just say the old men looked and loved?

I too like alliteration and can string it
like Christmas lights from line to line
but *make music, so the self-same sounds*
is excess, to my mind,
and *pulse pizzicati of Hosanna* – really?
I relish assonance as much as you,
she stood in the cool of spent emotions,
those oo-s cooing like doves
but you have gone too far with
simpering Byzantines and tambourines.

Don't get me wrong; I get it;
if music is feeling then poetry is feeling too,
a verbal music that attempts to bind
our senses to ideas, an image to a thought,
using all the tricks at our disposal
such as rhyme, that antique ruse,
but you overdo it with
quavering and wavering
and when you seek to vary
and make them off, you offend:

plays and praise, flame and shame.
Masculine or feminine, internal or otherwise,
rhymes lose their luster in the end
for sounds ignite one portion of the brain,
while meaning – more sister than lover – another.
Sound can sap the line of meaning
and lead us to say things that sound like truth,
the body lies; the body's beauty lives
    but aren't.

Mother of my poems, father of my thoughts,
my first love and with luck, my last,
images come easy – stone, water, light.
Alas, sight is not vision.
Metaphor, that bedrock of poetry,
serves the purpose of joining this and that,
but *death's ironic scrapings*
and *the viol of her memory*
are not exactly brilliant or exact.
Simile, its squire, limps along,
its *refrain like a willow swept by rain*
and irony, that cat's paw,
last refuge of the lazy,
fortress of the skeptical,
dishes up small portions of significance
like over-cooked and over-spiced
blini au saumon fume.
Irony annoys me, my own and yours,
for it lets the horrors of the world
off the hook and self-satisfied
moves on to look at something else.

As ceremony hides the heart's emotion
so rhetoric, the will at work,
conceals four verities of life
– birth, love, labor, death –
which is why I say in un-ironic terms
that truth is served by clarity
and simplicity is best.

Who am I kidding?
All art is made of rhetoric
trying to rise above rhetoric and failing,
striving to express what is eternal in the mind
but dying in the throes of fashion
and so, while I resist it, poorer,
I miss it and return to it as to a woman
who betrayed but loved me,
and vice versa, and all forgiven,
    marry.

Rhetoric

rhetoric, the will at work. Yeats' condescending remark: "rhetoric is will doing the work of imagination."

> Just as my fingers on these keys
> Make music, so the selfsame sounds
> On my spirit make a music, too.

> Music is feeling, then, not sound;
> And thus it is that what I feel,
> Here in this room, desiring you,

> Thinking of your blue-shadowed silk,
> Is music. It is like the strain

Waked in the elders by Susanna:

Of a green evening, clear and warm,
She bathed in her still garden, while
The red-eyed elders, watching, felt

The basses of their beings throb
In witching chords, and their thin blood
Pulse pizzicati of Hosanna.

II

In the green water, clear and warm,
Susanna lay.
She searched
The touch of springs,
And found
Concealed imaginings.
She sighed,
For so much melody.

Upon the bank, she stood
In the cool
Of spent emotions.
She felt, among the leaves,
The dew
Of old devotions.

She walked upon the grass,
Still quavering.
The winds were like her maids,
On timid feet,
Fetching her woven scarves,
Yet wavering.

A breath upon her hand
Muted the night.
She turned—
A cymbal crashed,
And roaring horns.

III

Soon, with a noise like tambourines,
Came her attendant Byzantines.

They wondered why Susanna cried
Against the elders by her side;

And as they whispered, the refrain
Was like a willow swept by rain.

Anon, their lamps' uplifted flame
Revealed Susanna and her shame.

And then, the simpering Byzantines
Fled, with a noise like tambourines.

IV

Beauty is momentary in the mind—
The fitful tracing of a portal;
But in the flesh it is immortal.

The body dies; the body's beauty lives.
So evenings die, in their green going,
A wave, interminably flowing.
So gardens die, their meek breath scenting
The cowl of winter, done repenting.
So maidens die, to the auroral
Celebration of a maiden's choral.

Susanna's music touched the bawdy strings
Of those white elders; but, escaping,
Left only Death's ironic scraping.
Now, in its immortality, it plays
On the clear viol of her memory
It makes a constant sacrament of praise.
       Wallace Stevens

I Left The House One Day

It was a hot, a boiling day without a cloud or breeze,
mother you remember how it was that summer
in the country. I left the house and headed down
the sandy street and saw a gypsy sitting on the ground.
His face was dark and sweaty from the heat.
Above him, on a wall, a monkey dressed in red skirt
and orange blouse, a leather collar with a chain
that led to the ragged man below.
Her back arched high, she bent her balding head
to a dish of water and drank greedily.
Suddenly she seized the dish
and swept it off the wall, then, seeing me,
she rose and offered me her black wet little hand.
It was a gentle gesture. I have shaken hands
with poets, well-born, merchants,
but never one like this, filled with dignity and grace
and sweetness. She gazed into my eyes with such sorrow
and affection, even wisdom, that in recognition
of our sisterhood, I yearned to set her free.
In that moment a cloud crept across the sun,
thunder clapped. The gypsy rose, brushed off his pants,
thumped his tambourine, and walked off,
the monkey rocking rhythmically on his shoulder.
I knew then mother it was right for me to leave
the house and Borya and not return.

I Left The House One Day

My poem is adapted from a poem by Vladislav Khodasevich.
He was born in 1886, a Lithuanian Jewish poet of Russian

upbringing and education. He went into self-exile at age 36, first to Berlin, then to Paris. His audience was the small quarrelsome community of exiles. He died at age 53, practically unknown.

His poem, called *The Monkey*, is typical of the way he used a personal experience to illuminate a historic moment. In this case it was the day WWI broke out in Russia. He mentions Darius fleeing Alexander and drinking from a puddle in the road. I've changed the narrator from male to female and imagined her as a Russian woman on the day she is leaving her house and husband for good.

Seeing The World

Tired of my yellow teeth and graying hair,
I'll chose the highway and the low way,
go somewhere squalid and dangerous
and be new there and hidden,
go for anonymous women
and days filled with words and a healing wound.

Cool or cold-blooded I'll slide smoothly
down an alley and through to the room
where men are devoured.

Do I do right though?
I have an eye that doesn't see
and an eye that barely sees
but if I see inward then I'll see the world.

Seeing The World

>one collapses and surrenders
>not out of choice
>or lack of intelligence
>or bad teeth
>or bad diet.
>
>one surrenders
>because that's the best movie
>around.
>
>>Bukowski

The Clack Of The Dice

> *He chucked up everything*
> *And just cleared off*
> Philip Larkin

And I did!
Chucked up everything
and just cleared out.
Not once but
    over and over
by bus, train, ship, on foot
and he's right
    it left me flushed and stirred
with thoughts of fucking in one town
and falling down drunk in another.

In Ghana it was palm wine,
in Morocco red, ouzo in Greece,
but in Baja it was rum.
After the third drink I heard footsteps
and the clack of the dice.

One night I stood on the middle deck
of a shabby freighter
and watched a little French liner
slip by on its Atlantic run,
its silver and golden lights shining.

Stranded in Texas, I turned north
toward Hondo, the mud house of ardor
that draws the sky down, to a wild bird
of air and flesh, a desert rose
waiting for me on the edge of the stream.

The Clack Of The Dice

>Sometimes you hear, fifth-hand,
>As epitaph:
>He chucked up everything
>And just cleared off,
>And always the voice will sound
>Certain you approve
>This audacious, purifying,
>Elemental move.
>
>. . .
>
>He walked out on the whole crowd
>Leaves me flushed and stirred,
>Like Then she undid her dress
>Or Take that you bastard;
>Surely I can, if he did?
>
>>Larkin

A man going home his hair flecked with white.
The blue clouds, the mountain berries
black as beads of lacquer,
the mouse folding its paws together,
all elate me.
When I arrive the boy seeing his dad
turns his back and weeps.
His feet are dirty.
The two little girls are in the bedroom
in dresses cut and sewn so often
that the flowers birds and sky
run together.
"How could I have forgotten
to bring you something?"

as I hand out silk, rouge and toys –
my wife's thin face begins to glow again.
In the morning our silly girls comb their hair
exactly like their mother's and make up their faces
in what we call the two-handed smear.
Yet I am sick; I have been vomiting at night.
And how do I bring up the subject
of how to make a living?
                              after Tu Fu

Canto Hondo

Here, at this longitude,
there is an abundance of light
even during a storm
but once or twice a year
a thick fog fills the valley.
As it lifts, a horse emerges standing by a fence,
then a high pile of sweet-smelling piñon
and a trailer and then through patches of bright fog
radiant spaces.

In the spring a hoe, clippers, eight shovels
in the right hands is magnificent.
The acequia runs for eight months
like blood without valves.

Dust devils meander up the road
and the little river gleans through the cottonwoods,
the lowest, loveliest thing in the valley.

In the summer we see blue mountains
and the green sees us. A gust of wind
blows rain into the bedroom
and onto the floor, which shines.

One September we had two feet of snow.
Birds lowered their temperatures.
She swept ants out the door.

The first gray of evening is filled with wings,
bats leaving their caverns
echoing their prey in flight.
The stumps in the field are moving
but our shadows have fled.

After the horns and lights of a wedding caravan
two guitars, a fiddle sounding like insects,
our shoes dusty from dancing.

An old man who sleeps with his Bataan metal
and at eight in the morning a man
leaning against the wall of the bar,
his face ravaged by drink.

A farmer is tied to the cross
for the religion of Christ and the whip.
There is blood on the ceiling
of the morada on the hill.

In this town sprawled flat, one step up from mud,
weeds are growing in the cracks of the basketball court,
the nets have been stolen for catching trout in the ditches.

The people here don't have a name
for the wind from the west
or if they do they haven't told me.
They could call it Señor Perverse
because in the morning it is sweet
with hay and manure but by noon
its kiss is a little rough and
the pond is trembling with excitement
and by two it is blowing hard,
shaking the poplars.
It announces rain that doesn't come
and we would cry Please
Señor Perverse if it had a name.

There is cactus, broom, fruit trees, a kitchen garden
and where the road bends, wild roses

and thickets of blackberries.
We wonder that such rocky soil supports so much life.

The horizons locked into light
the light – always the light
and blue sheets of rain
gliding to the west.

High in the hills, on cliffs and precipices,
there are petroglyphs, whorls and spirals
without shadows or feelings,
not art, not magic, but as timeless
as the rock permits.

When we throw seeds to the finches
the magpies swoop down.
The magpies and jays of this world want everything
and bees freeze in the icy air.

On rainy days the house is blurred like a photograph
and wet ashes like glue smear the doorstep.
The outhouse of weathered wood
sits like a wounded soldier waiting to die.

In the fall wasps sip at our spills of wine,
tiny red lakes on the blue table,
yellow wasps matching the yellow of the cottonwoods.

Here, on this property that has possessed me,
her ashes are in a metal box under the cedar tree,
gold tarnished to silver.

Our primitive house of joy has a foundation
of stones. The space under the house
is home to skunks snakes grubs and ants.

The ceremonies of spiders in the corners,
mica gleaming in the clay walls,
chainsaw oiled and sharpened
squatting in the corner like a praying mantis.

I danced with him on my feet,
slow dancing the four step with him on my feet
and she nestled in my arms
as we sang Sesame Street songs,
their tiny flesh mingling with mine.

I loved them early and learned
to love them even more.
That came with the house.

Phaedra glued little silver stars on the ceiling
of their room. She collected rosehips for our colds.
The way the bed was, we could see the sun rise
and the moon rise and an orange planet.

Home for a visit, Sara explained that thunder
is a sheet of metal and blood red silk.
She listened to mice behind the walls
and rain on the metal roof.

A blue wind rose in the dawn.
When Zander woke that's the morning waking.
Kettle hissing, magpies crying,
he split aspen that shone brightly
and the pieces went flying to land in the snow.

The little river, orchard, dirt road, the house,
we thought of them as ours, as one body
and us four embedded in it.
But drought and wind and time itself . . .

And yet the river, orchard, road, the house
exist in us as memory, part of us forever,
as one body.

Us Four

Canto Hondo

Arroyo Hondo, a small farming community ten miles north of Taos, New Mexico, was settled by Hispanic farmers. For over 130 years, from its founding in 1815 to World War II, it was the center of the universe for its residents. Electricity came in the 1940s, the first Anglos in the early 60s, and the main road was paved around 1980. In 2020 the village contains a post office and a minimarket attached to a bar.

The people here don't have a name for the wind. Inspired by a poem by Jorge Carrera Andrade, but I am unable to find it.

The souls of all my loved ones have flown to the stars.
Thank heaven there's no one left for me to lose.
Now I'm finally free to cry.
The day is full of echoes that sound like songs.

A silver willow reflected in the waters of September.
My silent shadow slides to me.
Many lyres hang in the branches
and lo – there's still room for mine.
The rain, struck by sunlight, brings me
memories that console me.
                    Akhmatova

Bright moonlight is shining like frost
on the wooden floor.
I raise my head to look at the moon.
Then I lower my head
and I think of home.
                    Li Po

Where The Piñon Jays Gather

I took the children to the dump to learn to shoot
a .22 and .38. There were green bottles there,
perfect as targets, and tin cans already punctured
with bullet holes, smooth on entry, ragged on exit.
I taught them the rules:
>never point a gun at a person
>never walk in front of the shooter
>keep the safety on until ready to shoot

the rules that had been drummed into me as a child.
I didn't mention my own personal rule:
>if you point a gun at someone shoot him.

The tin cans jumped, the green bottles and blue ones
shattered.

Once, instead of the dump, we went to a ravine
out in the mesa and there was a rusted Nash
Rambler, a mattress with cigarette burns
and a midsized mutt with brown fur
and no eyes, its teeth the color of peonies.
I wanted to say something comforting.
Instead: The world's no different.
Have no doubt that this is how it ends.

Where The Piñon Jays Gather

>Once at sunset Jesus and his disciples
>were on the road outside the walls of Zion
>when suddenly they came to where the town
>for years had dumped its garbage: burnt mattresses
>from sickbed, broken pots, rags, filth
>And there, crowning the highest pile, its legs

pointing at the sky, lay a dog's bloated carcass;
such a stench rose up from it that all the disciples,
hands cupped over their nostrils, drew back as one man.
But Jesus stood there, and He gazed so closely
at the carcass that one disciple called out from a distance,
"Rabbi, don't you smell that dreadful stench?
How can you go on standing there?"
Jesus, His eyes fixed on the carcass, answered:
"If your breath is pure, you'll smell the same stench
inside the town behind us, but Look how that dog's teeth glitter
in the sun: like hailstones, like a lily, beyond decay,
a great pledge, mirror of the Eternal,
but also the harsh lightning-flash, the hope of Justice!"

            Angelos Sikelianos

Neither Of Us Running

A gutted pickup in the weeds, its glass is gone,
its eyes gouged out, just a rusted metal frame.
We call it dead man's truck and say it's haunted.
When the first snow falls and frames its form
it's shrunken, blind and beautiful.

Seats sagging, our souls detached,
neither of us running, we sit
in the weeds throughout the day
and sleep through nights
dreaming of highways.

Snakes Shed Their Skin

There are so many poems about remembrance
of things past, regrets and joys,
embraces and the dead, *les neiges d'antan*.
Equal to the moment, music
in the garden vibrates in the mind,
violets live within the senses that they quicken.

I remember the smell of gun oil
in the barn, the corsage pungent on her chest,
her name was Jill, her skin tacky to the touch,
the gypsy's fiddle in the back streets of Toledo,
the heavy snows of '73 and the way the ocean
moved like blue marble and later turned to lettuce-green.

But the snows have vanished,
birds leave no trace in air,
whales move on, and faithful
to themselves winds leave no tracks.
They teach us to refuse to mourn,
to forget, fly on and disappear.

Snakes Shed Their Skin

    April is the cruelest month, breeding
    Lilacs out of the dead land, mixing
    Memory and desire, stirring
    Dull roots with spring rain.
    Winter kept us warm, covering
    Earth in forgetful snow, feeding
    A little life with dried tubers.
    Summer surprised us, coming over the Starnbergersee

With a shower of rain; we stopped in the colonnade,
And went on in sunlight, into the Hofgarten,
And drank coffee, and talked for an hour.
Bin gar keine Russin, stamm' aus Litauen, echt deutsch.
And when we were children, staying at the arch-duke's,
My cousin's, he took me out on a sled,
And I was frightened. He said, Marie,
Marie, hold on tight. And down we went.
In the mountains, there you feel free.
I read, much of the night, and go south in the winter.

Eliot

Better the flight of birds passing
and leaving no trace
than creatures leaving tracks.
Remembering betrays nature,
what's past is nothing.
Pass on bird, pass on and teach me how.

Pessoa

Best Poem Ever

Sitting outside with loose papers on my lap,
a gust blew the top two pages away.
It was a poem that contained some creatures
and the usual clouds and mists
and how fossils feel about mountains.
Like a Borges story, it contained the past and future
and how time distorts yet fuels our ability to love.
I jumped up and chased it down the road,
the poem containing metaphysical doubts
about existence, my own and yours,
and how everything doesn't mean anything.
There was a buzzing hornet
and Diogenes' mordant laughter
and it listed the questions that answer themselves
– Will I be born? Do I crave applause?
But it was gone, my best poem ever,
eaten by cactus or the wind.

Best Poem Ever

Best Poem Ever was inspired by Borges' story *The Aleph*. The Aleph is a point in space that contains all other points. Anyone who gazes into it can see everything in the universe from every angle simultaneously, without distortion, overlapping, or confusion.

I saw the teeming sea; I saw daybreak and nightfall; I saw the multitudes of America; I saw a silvery cobweb in the center of a black pyramid; I saw a splintered labyrinth (it was London); I saw, close up, unending eyes watching themselves in me as in a mirror; I saw all the mirrors on earth and none of them reflected me; I saw in a backyard of Soler Street the same tiles that thirty years before I'd seen in the entrance of a house in Fray Bentos; I saw bunches of grapes, snow, tobacco, lodes of metal, steam; I saw convex equatorial deserts and each one of their grains of sand.

Borges

It was a hot day and when I ran into Tu Fu
wearing a big straw hat I asked
"Tu Fu, how come you've grown so thin?
Are you in agony over one of your poems?"

Li Po

How Miraculous
The Music

From The Daily Courant

At 8 evening Wednesday, July 17, 1717, the King took water at Whitehall in an open barge and went up the River to Chelsea. Many other Barges with Persons of Quality attended, and so great a Number of Boats, that the whole River in a manner was cover'd. A City of London Barge was employ'd for the Musick, wherein were 50 instruments of all sorts, who play'd all the Way the finest Suites, compos'd express for this Occasion, by Mr. Hendel. At Eleven his Majesty went a-shore at Chelsea where a Supper was prepar'd, which lasted till two; after which, his Majesty came again into his Barge, and return'd the same Way, the Musick continuing to play entire twice more, till he landed.

Mostly right, the Courant, what with King George the First
and all, just past eight we pushed off into the tide
that raced upstream, no need for sail or oar
on that strong surge, His barge ahead and ours behind,
lesser boats with commoners and courtiers
and many others on all sides.

But not fifty that was commissioned, because first horn
and trumpet drank the very day and fell down
and third flute caught the bloody flux, so forty-seven:
flutes, trumpets, horns and so forth,
plus, against His taste, for He didn't like them,
violins that our maestro sneaked aboard

and I the second oboe proud to be amongst his orchestra
these seven years and know his wishes
and his want to please His Majesty with sound reason,
for He had been distraught of late with wife, unloving
and unloved, and with the Prince whose airs
were coupled with ambition.

Our conductor lost no time, raised his arm
and we began, a stately overture to lull the crowd
and we were off a bit, mistiming, distracted
by the festive flags and flaming torches
that burned in air and water.
Then we got our footing with a waltz from France
and a duple time bourrée Italian
and the lively hornpipe dance native to these Isles.
Our sarabande was rough, our gigue fine,
rigaudon the best we ever did, merriment made manifest
while our leader, known for melancholy,
was aglow with how miraculously his music
carried over water to the King.

At supper we repeated the more delicate of suites,
then back down toward Whitehall
and the mistress He adored. We played the music
all again and twice, four times in all,
the Royals ahead and we behind near three o'clock,
our maestro saying louder louder lads
as we wilted but exulted in the knowledge
that we were joining joy and sorrow
in the sailor's jig and the formal minuet.

Thus the evening ends, undressed torches put to bed,
flags furled and banners laid to rest.
His Highness raised his hand one German to another
in appreciation and in gratitude
to leave intrigues and griefs behind,
and our Handel's face was flush with triumph
for the King had said for all to hear
that He was happy and the music made him so.

From The Daily Courant

The Daily Courant, Britain's first daily newspaper, published an account of the premier of George Frideric Handel's Water Music on July 18, 1717.

the King. King George I, a German who was King of England, was fifty-seven at the time; Handel, also German, was thirty-two.

but not fifty. One report suggests that the King wanted a hundred musicians but no barge was large enough. The ambassador from Prussia reported that the instruments consisted of trumpets, horns, oboes, bassoons, flutes, violins and basses. A baroque orchestra would normally have included a harpsichord and timpani, but it would have been difficult to fit these onto the barge.

the bloody flux. Dysentery.

distraught of late with wife. After King George had his marriage to Sophia Dorothea dissolved, he imprisoned her in style in her native Celle, where she lived for the next thirty years. The King's mistress Melusine von der Schulenburg, with whom he had three daughters, acted as his hostess until his death.

the Prince with airs. It was rumored that the trip up the Thames with a trailing orchestra was designed to compete with the Prince and heir-apparent, whose lavish parties and dinners were drawing too much attention.

Listening To Dvořák's

cello concerto thinking
it would resurrect feelings
I had when I loved music
and a slim blond girl,
but I feel nothing that resembles bliss.

I go outside and outside is empty
of Dvořák and his triumphs and losses.
Gray ripples of light shine on the dust.
The sun burns the wind
and the wind scores the earth.

I spent time in Dvořák's music
and prefer mine of sun and wind.
I spent time in the real world
and prefer mine of dust and light.

Listening To Dvořák's

The Cello Concerto in B minor, Op. 104, is the last solo concerto by Antonín Dvořák. It was written in 1894 while he was in New York City serving a third term as the Director of the National Conservatory. The third movement is a tribute to his sister-in-law, Josefina Kaunitzova, who had written him a letter saying she was seriously ill. The slow, wistful section, before the triumphant ending, quotes the song "Leave Me Alone," a favorite of hers. The finale, he wrote, "should close gradually with a diminuendo like a breath . . . then there is a crescendo, and the last measures are taken up by the orchestra, ending stormily. That was my idea, and from it I cannot recede." She died in May 1895.

I Can Taste It

The suites for cello.
They taste like nothing earthly.
They taste like love.

Small black olives cloak the ground.

A smoky village.
We sweep the wooden planks
of pinewood worn down
by us for fifty years.

The cello's sound from deep
within our house of innocence
and purpose swells to something darker
than death's rattle, something deeper
than the echoes of our joy.

The ocean paces to and fro,
its hidden currents colder than the surface

then fireworks, a dance,
a holiday of cakes and spirits,
meals on wooden tables,
men and women dancing
in potato fields.

A track through aspens,
golden leaves and flashing butterflies.

We sail beyond the dazzle of the ship lanes
to the leaping mammals –
quick, before the cello's music disappears

I can taste it . . .

I Can Taste It

For me there is only one concrete proof for the existence of God: the music of Johann Sebastian Bach.
Cioran

She played Bach. I don't know the names of the pieces, but I recognized the stiff ceremonial of the frenchified little German courts and the sober, thrifty comfort of the burghers, and the dancing on the village green, the green trees that looked like Christmas trees, and the sunlight on the wide German country, and a tender coziness; and in my nostrils there was a warm scent of the soil and I was conscious of a sturdy strength that seemed to have its roots deep in mother earth, and of an elemental power that was timeless and had no home in space.
W. Somerset Maugham

The Dance

Zoltán Kodály's Duo for Violin and Cello Op. 7 was written in 1914 and first performed in 1918. It is the rare piece written for cello and violin, as these are so similar.

How dare he couple them, so similar
        and different
similar in color – bright
        different in texture – dark
not twins
        two butterflies twined around
                each other's flight
each seeks the other
        then they switch
                and flee the scene
like men in ugly hats and
        girls with ribbons in their hair
a thorny heart
     and one who soars
but which is which?
      is it marriage or divorce?
              they climb together
     only to fall out
  one gets the girl
        the other gets the gold
We die
     and fly from earth
  yet skies move in many ways
blue air emerges from the cloud
        and children play to Magyar songs.
        Mark how one string,

       sweet husband to another,
                    strikes each and each
    one and two
      and world is three
sweets with sweets war not
         joy delights in joy.

The Dance

Children play to Magyar songs. Kodály, along with Béla Bartók, was the premiere collector of Hungarian folk music, both songs and dances.

> Music to hear, why hear'st thou music sadly?
> Sweets with sweets war not, joy delights in joy:
> Why lov'st thou that which thou receiv'st not gladly,
> Or else receiv'st with pleasure thine annoy?
> If the true concord of well-tuned sounds,
> By unions married, do offend thine ear,
> They do but sweetly chide thee, who confounds
> In singleness the parts that thou shouldst bear.
> Mark how one string, sweet husband to another,
> Strikes each in each by mutual ordering;
> Resembling sire and child and happy mother,
> Who, all in one, one pleasing note do sing:
> Whose speechless song being many, seeming one,
> Sings this to thee: 'Thou single wilt prove none.
>   Shakespeare

I Wake To Waves And Voices

The world is infused with voices
and the remnants of music
is bathed in shapeless winds whistling over crops
and damp winds hissing over endless waves

and voices that move off half dead and naked
and winds at night worrying the doors and windows
and voices not mine but for me
all saying something different and the same

and winds heavy with dust and winged seeds
stirring the last of the embers
and voices of the waves undressing the light.

I Wake To Waves And Voices

Music lovers are familiar with Debussy's *La Mer*, but his *Nocturnes*, composed four years earlier, are equally fascinating and, at the time, with their shifting harmonies, as revolutionary. He wrote, "I am more and more convinced that music, by its very nature, is something that cannot be cast into a traditional and fixed form. It is made up of colors and rhythms."

Nocturnes consist of three parts, which he describes as: "*Nuages,* renders the slow movement of the clouds fading away in gray tones tinged with white; *Fêtes* offers the vibrating atmosphere of a festival of music and luminous dust; and *Sirènes* depicts the sea and its countless rhythms and the waves silvered with moonlight, the mysterious song of the sirens as they laugh and pass on."

Errico Beyle, Milanese

Night, and the town perfumed with jasmine
and seeped in the sounds of drunken soldiers
looting stores when I walk to the little Teatro Nuovo
to hear Cimarosa's Il Matrimonio Segreto.
Caroline loves Pasolino and they marry in secret
but Fidelma also loves Pasolino
and Count Robinson is to marry Elisetta but loves Caroline
and there's scheming and suffering and the lead actress
has a front tooth missing but the vibrant music
is sublime and fills my soul with such joy that joy
    becomes my goal in life.

I arrived a solemn boy and left a man whose greed
for happiness was absolute. I had been happy
several times before, in the hills above the town of Rolle
with the lake shimmering to the peals of church bells,
and watching Mélanie bathing in the river
naked or not quite naked,
and sitting under an elm at a little table in Der Grüne Jäger
writing the beginning of a book,
but none of these compare to the rapture
of Cimarosa's music or that night
in the little theater in Novaro
when I learned that art must be the substance of my days
    and love my nights.

Errico Beyle, Milanese

Henri Beyle, who published under the name Stendhal, was seventeen, a lieutenant who could barely ride a horse or handle a saber, when he heard *Il Matrimonio Segreto* (The Secret

Marriage) for the first time. For him that experience, involving a confluence of the senses, the heart and the mind, surpassed later success and gain and became the most memorable of his life.

Cimarosa was regarded in his day as the greatest composer of opera buffa but his work fell out of favor after his death, only to have it resurrected in recent years with productions of his operas and the recognition that they influenced Mozart.

Rolle. Overlooking Lake Geneva, in sight of the snow-covered Alps. Beyle had been reading Rousseau's *La Nouvelle Héloïse* and under its influence was in a heightened state of rapture.

Novaro. In the hills of Lombardy, twenty miles west of Milan.

Der Grüne Jäger (the Green Huntsman) was a pub in Brunswick that had special significance for Beyle. It is the title of the first chapter of his unfinished novel *Lucien Leuwen.*

In 1820, age thirty-seven, while living in Milan, Beyle wrote the words for his own headstone.

Errico Beyle
of Milan
lived, wrote and loved.
He adored
Cimarosa, Mozart and Shakespeare
and died in the year
18__.

The Raga

starts sluggishly
with long chords of contemplation
because life is a drag
and we have time enough for it.
It picks up speed and energy as the sitar
becomes a full-bodied cloud with silver lining,
the tabla the sun breaking through.
The musicians trade secrets,
swap jokes, take risks.
One hurries and the other, frantic,
hurries to catch up.

Ragas of rain, of dusty plains,
of footpaths and an empty room.
I hear two notes: a dove.
It's sunrise and the earth
is rinsed in morning light.
The tabla leaps beyond the sitar, and at noon
the peacocks call the cobras.
It is give and take, life and more life
and the moon in early evening.

Underneath, the tonic drone
sounds the basic note, the raga's ground.
It is relentless
It is not Western
it is barely human.

The estuary fills with tide
and the stars wheel outward and leave us.

The Raga

In the ancient music of northern India, a raga is a pattern of notes having characteristic intervals, rhythms, and embellishments used as a basis for improvisation. Each raga suggests a particular time of day and/or season. Ragas can "color the mind" and affect the emotions of the audience.

Cante Jondo
for voice only, adapted from flamenco songs

Every morning I go by
the rosemary bush
and ask it if there's a cure for love
because I'm dying of it

Anyone who hears me
will recognize my passion
It's not my mouth that speaks
It's my heart

There's a halo around the moon
My love has died
Singing the pain
the pain goes away

I'm off to Armenia
to drink with the animals
where no living soul
knows nothing of me

Cante Chico

God be with you when you're good
but best at other times to hide your head

At the top of Palomares mountain
some say single and others say a pair
I'll comb my hair in the mirror of the water
because I'm single and not a pair

Drunk?
I'm drunk? You must be joking!
But now that you mention it . . .
Because when I'm drunk
I can stop thinking about her

By twelve o'clock or one
when the wind begins to ebb
I'm drunk in the moonlight
    really stupefied

But I am seeing double
and that's not good
that's not good

I'm not that fond of blondes
they don't know how to kiss
I like dark-haired girls
whose kisses sweep away my sorrow

My love you come so late
and then you leave so quick
My heart doesn't need
such surgical efficiency

When we walk her dress
rubs up against me
and all of me, I mean all of me
shutters with desire

Cante Flamenco

Cante flamenco (flamenco singing) is one of the three components of flamenco, along with *toque* (playing the guitar) and *baile* (dance). The most serious and passionate are the cante jondo (cante grande), sung by both women and men accompanied only by clapping and tapping on a table. Cante chico is lighter and usually with guitar.

Risking Tickets

In the summer of 1960, age nineteen, I dropped out of college and made plans to go to Europe for a year of wandering and writing. I was listening to a lot of music, both pop and classical, and I especially loved Shostakovich's Cello Concerto No. 1, which had been written and recorded the previous year.
 For Mstislav Rostropovich, who first performed the concerto

Allegretto: Dawn
Still dark on the road driving to Bakersfield for a cup
of coffee in my Studebaker slim as she is and as fast,
faster than the empt fruit trucks I'm passing breakneck
on the one lane road with windows open radio too loud
pulsing dream lover dilly dilly lavender blue and Elvis
crooning about needing love tonight over wind-whipped
dead man's curve on Tejon Pass and forty miles
of bad road. No moon in June or wedding, not for her
who chose abortion. Bakersfield at dawn is flat fields
of meals for city tables, and back again driving on the road
before there was a highway five across town
through the early traffic risking tickets and why not,
moving forward like a sleepless shark to the beach
where it's still dawn and sit and look. Look – the waves –
climb higher and little shore birds racing from the surf
and then the sun and then to work in time.

Moderato: Dusk
This is the sad part, the lugubrious part, lying on my bed
of self-love listening to the cello and some songs about lonely
teardrops, take a message to Mary, teen angel, so young,
too young to understand, and the cello cuts in about a soul

being born and sorrow over how to be a man. Father, sisters,
lover, mother. Mom! she lights another cigarette and pours
another Scotch, her dusk in me, father is conducting
from his chair, the music holds a menace I don't understand
but father I understand, please forgive me. No sounds
except the cello plunking,moaning like an animal dying
beneath thorns and silent headlights swim across the wall
north to south, south to north as cars drift up
and down Stone Canyon.

Cadenza Attacca: Midnight
The silver smog is hidden in the dark, love is strange.
Lipstick on my collar, mack the knife, smoke gets in my eye,
only the lonely, cherry pie, coffee, true but lord we lied
to each other and to ourselves crawling on the café floor
and other loony stuff, it's disturbing. Weary, waiting,
for what? a donut to be glazed, my friend has not shown up,
wait an hour past the midnight hour, wondering who I'll be,
if I will, pen poised over howl without a book mark,
neon in the stasis of the window that reflects a youth,
a couple, and a drunk, in the city of illusions
retailed by the ounce.

Allegro con moto: Noon
Quick up the coast my girl and me past gated Malibu
to songs it's now or never, jimmy go, volare,
this is the day on one o one in the Studi yellow as a wasp
curving around curves past hobo fires beneath the pines
in the middle of the day, rolling on past sparking green
green waves rolling in, to the sands of Zuma
and down the beach where bees are serenely
violating salty bushes to the grove of sweet and sticky

eucalyptus bark peeling off white limbs where I meet
my thrill bang bang and the climax of my adolescence.
Sun and glittering sea and again bump bump in the dunes
one last time before I catch the ship headed
for Le Havre and to the old trains that travel into the future.

Risking Tickets

Shostakovich's concerto is scored for solo cello, two flutes, two oboes, two clarinets, two bassoons, one horn, timpani, celesta, and strings. The work has four movements in two sections, with movements two through four played without a pause:

      I.   Allegretto
     II.   Moderato
    III. Cadenza – Attacca
    IV. Allegro con moto

The concerto is widely considered to be one of the most difficult works for cello, along with the *Sinfonia Concertante* of Prokofiev, with which it shares certain features (such as the prominent role of isolated timpani strokes). Shostakovich said that "an impulse" for the piece was provided by his admiration for that earlier work.

Different Drum

Between my junior and senior year
I lived in my mother's garage
and across the street, a woman hanging
sheets and pillowcases
and the shirts and pants and underwear
of a man, a woman and boys and girls,
six lines of laundry,
a brunette, not much older than me,
a Mrs. Fields, my mother said
with just the slightest lift of her lip.
A hot summer, I lay in the room over the garage
and read St. Exupery's Wind, Sand and Stars,
Manzoni's The Betrothed, and listened to a tiny radio,
Herb Alpert's The Lonely Bull
and Linda Ronstadt's Different Drum.
A few birds were chirping, a car passed on the country road,
and I looked out and saw her in the yard
hanging laundry and feeding hens, a handsome woman
in a short-sleeved dress that revealed her thin arms
and hid her large bust.

    Hi, my name is Jim. I'm living across the street

From a height of weariness, she gave me a look that said:
    I know you college boy,
        and I ain't saying you ain't goodlooking
        but I ain't having it and you ain't getting any
        so go on home

In the evenings I sat with my mom
who listened to Scott Joplin's rags

and rattled the thin pages of the Times Literary Supplement
and let the ice melt in her glass of scotch
and let her cigarettes burn down.
Mrs. Fields and I could both hear an owl hooting in the night
and the rooster's cry in the morning.
At dawn I climbed to the roof of the garage
and looked at the last stars
and the slice of ocean shining in the west.

A second visit to the clothes lines,
the grass thinly surviving the children's feet,
a rabbit in a hutch (for meat)
a rooster and his hens (for eggs)
and panties and bras not in sight.
I learned a little: first name Donna,
her husband spent the week in San Fernando
repairing city buses,
two boys and a girl away at grandma's,
and I told her that I was back from Italy, majoring in Italian lit.,
she listened patiently and then, cracker grammar gone,
another look, that said:
> Can't you tell, I've got my doubts,
> I'm really tired and the world is rough
> and I am rough
> and here's the dirt: my belly is covered with stretch marks,
> so please stop making eyes at me,
> you'll live a lot longer

He played the piano in brothels, my mother said of Joplin,
and died at 49 of syphilis.
The summer got hotter, my room unbearable,

I could smell the road melting
and the dust on the avocado trees.
The sea was a long way away.

A third time, I saw an engine hanging
from the branch of a tree
and she had put on lipstick
and this look had a note of sadness:
> Don't get me wrong, I understand
> you want a woman who'll make you a man,
> but I'm not in the market for a boy who loves,
> and furthermore, you'll be leaving soon
> so – please – go.

Different Drum

Different Drum is a song written by Mike Nesmith and popularized in 1967 by the Stone Poneys featuring Linda Ronstadt.

Linda Ronstadt

Nights In White Satin

We sat in her courtyard and played cards and listened to moody blues stirring the leaves of the banana tree. She lit a Delicados sin filtro and laid down a trick and picked up a hash joint rolled with tobacco.

The floor tiles shrink and expand like breathing boxes.
Light flickers in my eye. I am gazing at her
but just what the truth is, no one can say.
It's just what we're going through
this woman, my friend?

Soft air is riding the satin. Cards lay discarded
like letters we've written never meaning to send.
Beauty I catch in the side of my eye,
tricks on the truth I cannot defend.

Although some try, they don't understand,
it's the future we've seen, a sweet ruin.
It's just what we are going through,
never reaching the end.

Nights In White Satin

Nights in White Satin is a 1967 song by the Moody Blues, on the album *Days of Future Passed*, written and composed by Justin Hayward.

The 17th Day, Partway

Divorced and lost with nothing left to lose
I loved her, then her and almost her
and then I loved *her*
and when it was time to part,
I went with her partway.
What led up to this was what
you'd expect. We met day one,
talked day two, and feeling good,
for feeling good was good enough for us,
made love day three.
Afterward we sat in the garden
and shared the secrets of our souls.

Day nine she drove us into the mountains
in her RV, cooked a meal,
yanked the table out and drove me into bed
because happiness, we said, was nothing if not free.

I said I'd go partway but by then I'd gone all the way
and fallen in love. It was in Oklahoma City
that I let her slip away and oh I forgot,
on the thirteenth day, stoned and drunk,
she dressed in my shirt and pants
and I dressed in her baggy blouse and baggy pants
and we went to a restaurant like that and got more drunk
and agreed I'd move to Montreal
and hold her body next to mine.

The 17th Day, Partway

Busted flat in Baton Rouge, waitin' for a train
And I's feelin' near as faded as my jeans
Bobby thumbed a diesel down, just before it rained
It rode us all the way to New Orleans

I pulled my harpoon out of my dirty red bandanna
I was playin' soft while Bobby sang the blues, yeah
Windshield wipers slappin' time, I was holdin' Bobby's hand in mine
We sang every song that driver knew

Freedom's just another word for nothin' left to lose
Nothin', don't mean nothin' hon' if it ain't free, no no
And, feelin' good was easy, Lord, when he sang the blues
You know, feelin' good was good enough for me
Good enough for me and my Bobby McGee

From the Kentucky coal mine to the California sun
There Bobby shared the secrets of my soul
Through all kinds of weather, through everything we done
Yeah, Bobby baby kept me from the cold

One day up near Salinas, Lord, I let him slip away
He's lookin' for that home, and I hope he finds it
But, I'd trade all of my tomorrows, for a single yesterday
To be holdin' Bobby's body next to mine

Me and Bobby McGee written by Kris Kristofferson, popularized by Janis Joplin in 1971.

MP3 On A Summer Day

I was born by the river sings Sam Cooke,
things are going to change
meaning for blacks but for me too,
are already changing.

Shimmering gamelan
sweet and sour raga
growl of cello and flight of violin,
Fats Domino finding his thrill on blueberry hill,
Then there is reggae and I am
out of the chair and moving shirtless
under the soaring cottonwoods,
clumsy on the ancient path
with its tiny yellow flowers
rooted below the wind

then really dancing
knees high
sweetness of the sun on my chest
and music and the flowers
that survive without rain
and the path blazing
and the cedar tree where
her ashes are buried
waving its branches,
waving them like arms.

MP3 On A Summer Day

My MP3 player isn't organized by genre so music of different genres comes up randomly.

I was born by the river in a little tent
Oh and just like the river I've been running ev'r since
It's been a long time, a long time coming
But I know a change gonna come, oh yes it will
It's been too hard living, but I'm afraid to die
'Cause I don't know what's up there, beyond the sky
It's been a long, a long time coming
But I know a change gonna come, oh yes it will
     Sam Cooke

I found my thrill
On Blueberry Hill
On Blueberry Hill
When I found you
The moon stood still
On Blueberry Hill
And lingered until
My dream came true
The wind in the willow played
Love's sweet melody
But all of those vows you made
Were never to be
Though we're apart
You're part of me still
For you were my thrill
On Blueberry Hill
     Fats Domino

He's In The Back Booth

in the dark with his wine,
a whisky sour, a beer buzz in the morning,
and all he wants to do is have some fun.
He's not the only one.
He's got it all, the sun the moon some stars
and chips and salsa and the backbar bottles
clinking in the tremor.

Anonymous and single, there you have it.
When the sun goes down it's death poured
out a bottle packaged as rebirth.
The past is swallowed by the present.
He thinks love takes many forms, and not-love too,
so he'd give birth to something late in life.
Too late?
Too late.
Too late to love.
Too late to hate.
He's not the only one.

He's In The Back Booth

    All I want to do is have a little fun before I die
    Says the man next to me out of nowhere
    It's apropos of nothing he says his name is William
    But I'm sure he's Bill or Billy or Mac or buddy

    And he's plain ugly to me, and I wonder if he's ever
    Had a day of fun in his whole life

    'Cause all I wanna do is have some fun

I got a feeling I'm not the only one
All I wanna do is have some fun
I got a feeling I'm not the only one
All I wanna do is have some fun
Until the sun comes up over
Santa Monica Boulevard

I like a good beer buzz, early in the morning
Billy likes to peal the labels from his bottles of bud
He shreds them on the bar then he lights up every match
In an over-sized pack letting each one burn
Down to his thick fingers before blowing and
Cursing them out, he's watching
The bottles of bud as they spin on the floor

Otherwise the bar is ours, the day and the night
And the car wash, too
The matches and the buds, and the clean and dirty cars
The sun and the moon

But, all I wanna do is have some fun
I got a feeling I'm not the only one

 Wyn Cooper, sung by Sheryl Crow in 1993.

Too late. Too late. Aschenbach thought. But was it too late? This step he had delayed to take might so easily have put everything in a lighter key, have led to a sane recovery from his folly. But the truth may have been that the aging man did not want to be cured, that his illusion was far too dear to him.
          Thomas Mann

The Proper Distance

The Proper Distance

About suffering, the Old Masters
may never have been wrong
but they didn't always agree.
Ovid for instance says the fisherman,
ploughman and shepherd looked up
and wondered what specks those were,
men or gods, flying through the sky,
while Bruegel's fisherman is fishing,
ploughman ploughing and shepherd herding.
It is Auden, modern master,
who says they see the falling boy
and turn away, having better things to do.

Ovid's is a full account,
of a fruitful island of bulls and acrobats,
a boy laughing while he thumbs the soft wax
and a father, fabulous inventor,
scolding the boy and kissing him
and saying don't fly too low
or the waves will soak the wings
and weigh you down
or too high, the sun will melt the wax.

Sailors sail on but look
who stopped to see:
Ovid borrowing from old myths,
Bruegel with palette and brush
overlooking field and sea,
and Auden, in a tweed jacket,
gazing at a painting in the Musée des Beaux Arts.

And I am writing about them
and you are reading this.
Where do we stand?
What is the proper distance from the suffering
of the boy who staggered in the sky
and from the father who heard his boy's cry
smothered by the sea and wept in anger/love
and circled helplessly and then flew on to Sicily
to his labyrinth of grief.

The Proper Distance

> About suffering they were never wrong,
> The old Masters: how well they understood
> Its human position: how it takes place
> While someone else is eating or opening a window
> or just walking dully along;
> How, when the aged are reverently, passionately waiting
> For the miraculous birth, there always must be
> Children who did not specially want it to happen, skating
> On a pond at the edge of the wood:
> They never forgot
> That even the dreadful martyrdom must run its course
> Anyhow in a corner, some untidy spot
> Where the dogs go on with their doggy life and the torturer's horse
> Scratches its innocent behind on a tree.
> In Breughel's Icarus, for instance: how everything turns away
> Quite leisurely from the disaster; the ploughman may

Have heard the splash, the forsaken cry,
But for him it was not an important failure; the sun shone
As it had to on the white legs disappearing into the green
Water, and the expensive delicate ship that must have seen
Something amazing, a boy falling out of the sky,
Had somewhere to get to and sailed calmly on

                        Auden

What Is The Proper Distance?

Poussin says step back far enough
to see the whole, a balanced world
of trees and marble, prayer and death.
The composition's cold as reason.
His is a brooding city rich in its indifference,
the insignificance of life matched by death's.
The winding path flows upward
to festivities, then the tomb of some rich
merchant, a temple of a nameless god,
and overarching all, the branches of an oak and sky.

As for loyal Phocion, a man of antique virtue,
victim of injustice, he's the tiny shrouded thing
being carted off, a man's life reduced
to a splash of white lead paint.

Is this what art is, a cool construct to ease the mind,
to offer clarity to chaos? His art says hemlock
always has the final say,
poor Phocion's life dwarfed by civic order
and his death by oak and sky.

What Is The Proper Distance?

Nicolas Poussin was called Pictor Philosophicus, painter-philosopher, because of his learning and the cast of his mind. His *Landscape with the Funeral of Phocion* exists in three versions. Phocion was an esteemed statesman and soldier in fourth century b.c. who was defamed, forced to drink hemlock, and denied burial in the city of Athens.

Susanna And The Elders

is an old story told in the Bible
to warn the girls and titillate the rabbis.
How old was she? Eleven, fifteen, twenty-one?
I imagine her thirteen with hips like a boy
and budding breasts
because that is what old men want,
a girl, but not a child.
I used to see them as desiccated and feeble
but now I know they are sixty-eight or so
with bellies and gray hair, still capable
but beginning to be strange with age.
One of them wants to look
more than he wants to love,
another to penetrate every orifice
orifice after orifice and never stop.
A third is almost indifferent;
he would prefer a boy.

Stevens has her cool in green water
but clothed in rhetoric,
more music than a living breathing woman.
Artemisia Gentileschi paints her
with wide hips but not excessive,
a fresh brunette who attracts
the light and lecher eyes,
a wife who thinks she knows the ways of love
because she loves her husband's soft black hair,
his voice, his chest . . .

and she loathes the elders
and is repulsed by the lewdness of their lust
and the things they say, first behind their hands
and then to her.

The Bible story is a court case – "she says, they say" –
until she trips them up
with some Talmudic nonsense
but that is not the part people remember.
It is the looking that excites us, and the being seen.

I create my own Susanna fresh from the desert,
black hair and dusky skin and soft gray eyes
who throws her clothes off
and lowers herself into the water
that is cool against her thighs,
naked as only a woman can be
and sings an ancient Hebrew song:
wife, woman, a little wild, even crazy
and spied upon, gives the evil eye to them
and struts home through the palm trees
proud, faithful, eager for her husband.
I would write a poem about her,
how she steps into the pool in the heat of midday,
birds singing in the trees, a breeze lifting her hair,
and she splashes water upward on her breasts
and wipes it downward off her hairless belly
and moans with pleasure,
not realizing how many painters and poets
in the Western world are watching her
and figuring how to make her.

Susanna And The Elders

Artemisia Gentileschi was an Italian Baroque painter considered to be one of the most accomplished seventeenth-century artists. She was producing professional work by the age of fifteen. Many of her paintings feature women from myths, allegories, and the Bible, including victims, suicides, and warriors. She was known for being able to depict the female figure with great naturalism.

Artemisia

Zeus, Besotted With Her Beauty

Was she a dreamer, innocent and unaware, too pure to touch,
or a harlot only in it for the gold? One has her sleeping
in a dreamy state, another hauling in cold coins.
It's Rembrandt who gets it right.

So it's a shock when a young man stabs his Danaë
in the groin, then splashes sulfuric acid on her face,
a second slop of it across her breasts,
a last flick of the jar on her belly.

Not angel or a whore, Rembrandt's woman,
ready for whatever's next, is delighted by the mist
that bathes her flesh in golden light.

Zeus, Besotted With Her Beauty

When the king of Argos was told by the Oracle that he would die at the hands of his grandson, he locked his daughter Danaë in a tower to prevent her from becoming pregnant. The tower, made of bronze, had no windows or doors, so that no man could enter, but the king did allow a narrow opening in the ceiling for light and air. Zeus, besotted by her beauty, flowed through the opening as a shaft of golden light and impregnated her.

    The moment was painted by Titian, Rembrandt, Correggio, Gentileschi and other Renaissance artists in a variety of interpretations. Rembrandt's painting depicts her as a real woman enjoying the attention. His painting, hanging in the Hermitage in St. Petersburg, was vandalized by a young Lithuanian in 1985.

Two Bacchae

Why did Velázquez paint them the way he did,
the god clothed in light but looking concerned,
the seedy drinkers drunk? It can't be just because
the King requested it and paid a hundred ducats.
Could it be an allegory of innocence and depravity
or how Greek myth, luminous and rich,
compares to the poverty of gritty Spain?
For these men are gritty, sodden, ominously
thinking they might have the boy.
He'd destroy them first, of course;
maybe that's his concern, that he'll
have to wipe them off the earth.

As for the other, Caravaggio's motives are much clearer,
his portrait of the rent boy with sly and misty eyes,
boyish flesh, and a slight sneer for the customer,
is so lush we wonder if he used a mirror
to paint what he loves the most, himself,
and portray his life amidst the grubby pillow
and the rotting fruit and a pomegranate
that is ripe to bursting.

Two Bacchae

Velázquez painted his Bacchus around 1628, clearly influenced by Caravaggio although not necessarily by his Bacchus painting, and perhaps by Rubens, who was visiting Madrid around the same time. His is a plump young man, glancing away from the drunk and somewhat sinister ruffians whom he has gotten drunk. His skin is pale, in contrast to the rough dark faces of the peasants.

Caravaggio painted his in 1595, when he was twenty-four. The young good-looking model may have been his lover, although he may have been a self-portrait, using a mirror.

> Now raise our glasses to the youth
> who invented song and dance.
> Troubles gone,
> we drown our sorrow in his praise.
> Life is dark. Let's dance and play
> and raise our glasses to young Bacchus
> who taught us how to love.
> Anacreon

They're Very Different, These Three Nudes

Titian's, with her roses and a sleeping dog,
is a bride waiting on her wedding night,
unfazed but a little apprehensive.

Goya's is another matter, a grown woman
who knows she's gorgeous.
Godoy loves her, so does Goya.
That smile! It seems to say:
You like what you see?

Manet's Parisienne has a black ribbon around her neck,
a red silk orchid in her hair, her frank stare
is bored, not disdainful but indifferent,
close to cold, and we can almost hear her:
Leave the money on the table.

Yet they are sisters, these three nudes.
Look at them and they look back.
They say in different ways I'm right here
and I am yours, but be careful what
you want, the woman that you see
understands your hunger and your fear.

They're Very Different, These Three Nudes

The names of the models are almost as erotic as the paintings. Titian's was probably Giuliana Varano, the bride of the Duke of Urbino, in which case the painting was commissioned to celebrate their wedding. Goya's was thought to be the Duchess of Alba, his friend and patron, but recent scholarship thinks it was Pepita Tudó, the mistress of Manuel de Godoy, the Queen's lover. Manet's Olympia was his favorite model,

Victorine Meurent, nicknamed La Crevette, the Shrimp, because of her petite stature. She was in her day a more successful painter than Manet.

The title of Titian's painting, the Venus of Urbino, was assigned to it much later; there is nothing classical or allegorical about it. The title of Goya's, La Maya Desnuda, reveals his fascination with the flamboyant lower-class girls who strutted around Madrid. Manet called his painting Olympia; no one seems to know why.

His Olympia was a *succès de scandale*. In the Salon des Refusés, the show of painters rejected by the official salon, it was "skyed," that is hung high on the wall, to lessen its shock, but the public, which loved and hated it, demanded that it be brought lower. Critics called her a harlot, a female gorilla. Two guards were posted to protect it, for there was a concern that someone might deface it, not because of the nudity but the vulgarity of displaying the reality of Paris love life.

Manet, a bourgeois gentleman to his toes, didn't see himself as a rebel. He longed for acceptance by critics and the public. His innovations came, not from any desire to be radical or even different, but from necessity. He painted the way he painted because that is how he painted.

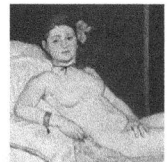

Olympia

Only Air Beneath Me
Goya speaking

She calls me Paco Goya and then laughs
because I cannot hear. Dressing like a maya,
of the common sort, she's a goose that doesn't
understand what life or death is.
She surrounds herself with cripples, senile clerics
and damaged misfits who leap to her whims.
She seems heartless but that is out of boredom.
I painted her exulting clothed and naked.

As for Leocadia, her laugh and eyebrows
and her splashing eyes once roused in me
the lust I felt for Rita Luna, the actress
who excelled in dagger roles. She was the mirror
of my lust, but in the face of fever
she grew practical, she wondered
who would get the house and orchard.
Peasant like, I deeded them to Mariano,
son of my son, warmth of my mornings.

They arose in me when I was lost
in fever and delirium, images
of sins and freaks. I died, music
and voices died with me.
I staggered out of illness
like a man out of the sea
and painted shrieks I could not hear,
the fearful faces of the godless
pressed against the superstitious pious,
matching those who torment

with those they torment.
The rooms were dark and I painted
with candles in my hat,
deaf as a stick painted as if blind.

Looking is seeing, drawing is breathing,
lines thin and thick, planes lit up
and drowned in shadow.
I drew things real, remembered
and imaginary, a beggar without legs,
a woman whose clothes are blowing,
Judith with the head of Holofernes,
a man eating leeks, a man picking
fleas off his dog, an ancient crone,
a Cossack and an old man on a swing.
An old man on a swing, This is me
deaf, almost blind, kicking up my crusty heels
higher than my head. I am past cares and wisdom,
feel a wicked sweetness like a child,
air prowling beneath my shirt
and only air beneath me.

Only Air Beneath Me

She calls me Paco. Referring to Maria Teresa Cayetana de Silva, 13th Duchess of Alba.

Leocadia. Leocadia Weiss, Goya's housekeeper/mistress who may have also been the mother of his daughter.

I drew things real, remembered. Goya spent his old age in exile in Bordeaux sitting in cafés and at home drawing whatever he saw or came to mind.

Le Suicidé

Because he was bored with loveless noons in loveless
rooms, the stains on the ceiling looked like yachts
            huddled together.

Curious about nothing, the execution
of himself was performed to end
the endless talking and rejoin
            the blessed void.

Was the artist mad when he painted him
with his legs dangling over the side of the bed
and his hand still holding the revolver,
            or merely morbid?

The whites of the shirt, the blacks of the pants, the reds
of the blood smeared on the shirt and the floor,
they are not to illustrate the horror of the act,
but are an incident of brush and palette, a display
of light and color. The corpse will soon be gone;
            Manet's art remains.

Le Suicidé

Le Suicidé, a small oil painting by Édouard Manet completed between 1877 and 1881, depicts a man in a shabby hotel room who has just shot himself. Unlike academic paintings of Socrates in protest, Cleopatra in despair, Chatterton in madness, Manet's painting is without moral or narration; it is as impersonal as a crime scene photo of a nameless man whose motive is of no interest. Adolphe Tabarant, Manet's early biographer, characterized it as "an incident of the palette," a detached study of light and color.

In his last years Manet limited himself to small still lifes of fruits and vegetables. His last exquisite paintings were of flowers in glass vases.

The Light At Daybreak

Monet saw well. He lived for painting poplars,
locomotive smoke at Gare Saint-Lazare
and rain at Étretat. He was in a hurry, out early
to catch the light as it revealed the world.
When light gathered in his eye he painted it
and as it changed, painted it again
and again, for light changed the way
a haystack looked, and it dawned on him,
how strange the world disclosed itself
as changing light, as if not light
but changing light defines the world.

In his middle years, Monet's reds grew rusty,
yellows became too yellow, blues too blue,
poplars greasy, flowers smeared.
He painted what he saw but scrapped them,
for he knew them wrong.

My eye without a lens
the other is crusted with a cataract.
Headlights are exploding stars,
trees are clouds of green,
near and far a hazy thing
and looking up, a growl of prop plane
and cries of birds devoured by the blue.

How modest my cloudy sight compared to his,
yet we share defects and distortions,
murky colors and corroded contours
and other ways of seeing badly
because of protein clumping on the lens.

His doctors said: have operations.
They pledged success.
He resisted for good reasons:
mistakes are made.

At first he roamed from Giverny
as far as Jeufosse, but he grew even older
and strayed close to home,
and finally, desperate, had the operation,
and it worked, successful in unexpected ways.

Since then procedures have evolved,
they slit the cornea, break the protein
into tiny pieces and suck them out,
and then, if all goes well,
fold the new acrylic lens and slide it in the eye
where it unfolds like a flower
focusing the world of stars and bees.

Yet I resist. I like the way I see
for how I see is me,
a line of shopping carts a gleaming dragon,
a fallen poplar white as ancient bones,
red willows as a burning bush,
a landscape fantastic in its error,
reality a construct of a poet's mind.

The painter sleeps massively and dreams
of being young or dead, of being young in love
when love was young, or dead down steep alleys
to the fallow fields below.

He rises in the dark and carries canvases
through the garden to a little craft on the stream
and works quickly, by starlight, arranging easels
and canvases in a row and his brushes,
tubes of paint and palettes.
He pushes off into the flow
and the night turns the color of clay.

The first canvas is for the first light that swallows the stars.
The second while Jupiter still gleams
and colors are nestled in the shadows.
The fourth is for the light scattered by mist.
The sixth for that shine that wakes the dragonflies.
The eighth is for liquid merged with light,
The tenth light stays longer than the rest
and the final light reveals the green dawn
and the red of blackbirds.

Back in the studio
he paints over two that don't please him,
throws another in the trash.
In the garden under an umbrella, old,
stuffed into himself, he eats a lunch
of soup, rabbit, fried potatoes,
a piece of cheese, and plums.
Three more he slashes into shreds.
He burns the rest, watching with a bitter
laugh the acrid light they make
not at all like the light at daybreak.

In old age, certain subjects rose before him,
things that he himself had built or planted,
the Oriental bridge, the garden of wisteria,
mimosa, lilies, lilies most of all
as they floated in water that reflected sky.
His days of troubled seeing taught him
what is far is not as real as what is near
and what is near is closest to the heart,
and if repeated, realer yet.
Sky and water came to mirror one another
and that is what he painted at the end,
a world made One,
his sight replaced by vision.

The Light At Daybreak

as if not light but changing light defines the world. In 1891 Monet began to paint the same scene repeatedly viewed from the same position in space but at different times of day. He chose as his subjects the cathedral in Rouen, haystacks, and later, lilies in a pond, and these came to exist, well before Einstein, in time as well as in space. He often had an assistant to help him prepare for the morning's work on the stream near his home in Giverny. They lined up as many as fourteen canvases on the little boat and unwrapped them. Then, handling the long brushes dexterously, he began to paint. He painted with a full brush, and moved quickly from canvas to canvas as the light changed. He always had a subject: a bridge, trees, the famous lilies. I have imagined that what he wanted to do, and increasingly moved toward doing, was to paint light itself in all of its transformations.

In the same vein, throughout his life, Goethe had a deep fascination for the physical and metaphorical effects of light.. While being now best remembered for his literary works, he himself believed the scientific treatise *The Theory of Colors*, which he published in 1810, was his most important achievement. He spent the evening before his death discussing optical phenomena with his daughter-in-law.

All of the above might lead us to believe that his celebrated deathbed cry of *Mehr Licht!* (More light!) was a plea for increased enlightenment before dying. The truth appears to be more prosaic. What he actually said was: "Do open the shutter of the bedroom so that more light may enter." There is, by the way, some debate whether his last words were not, in fact, "Come my little one, and give me your paw."

> I saw Eternity the other night,
> Like a great ring of pure and endless light,
> All calm, as it was bright
> > Henry Vaughn

> Light breaks where no sun shines;
> Where no sea runs, the waters of the heart
> Push in their tides;
> And, broken ghosts with glow-worms in their heads,
> The things of light
> File through the flesh where no flesh decks the bones.
> > Dylan Thomas

The Photographer

shot in fog, rain, sunshine and lack of it,
in the worse weather, at twilight. He chose
sentimental subjects like a begging fiddler and his boy
and in Paris, went through a surreal phase
and later in America, formal compositions.
He loved the chairs in Paris parks, their elegance
and shadows, a couple drenched by a sudden spring shower
and the peaked roofs of villages parked in rows
like sailboats, his people smudges
in dark clothes walking in the streets
hurrying as if life was important.

The Photographer

André Kertész, Hungarian photographer, born in 1894 and raised in Budapest, worked as a stock broker while photographing with an ICA box camera. He moved to Paris age 31 where, to survive, he worked as a photojournalist, but he always practiced his art, now using a 35 mm Leica. He spent much of this time in cafés waiting for inspiration. He moved to America ten years later and spoke a hybrid language, Hungarian, French, English and Yiddish, and no matter how many commissions and awards he received, he felt unappreciated and discouraged; it shows in his American work, as if he were solving compositional problems.

Kertész was deeply reserved, and his photographs don't invade people's personal space; they lack the aggression inherent in most photos. He loved his zoom lenses and took many photos from above or from a distance. Technically he was a master at cropping but it is not his technique that distinguishes his art. His talent was an ability to combine observing and feeling and then to convey that experience with tranquility. He found the rhythms of a scene and the patterns in the eye. It was Cartier-Bresson who provided the most fitting tribute: "Each time André Kertész's shutter clicks, I feel his heart beating."

The Idiot-Savant Says

I'm a tranquil soul comfortable with stealing from circuses
and spas and I lie. I'm such a liar, you know it's true.
I lie and in the lies there's life for life is truer than the truth.
Yet life, life without art, is a teeming stomach that digests,
a hollow heart that pumps, it's mud huts
huddled in the ghastly shadow of a church.

Anything can be the seed, Sordo's slouch, Ekberg's hair,
Aimée's cheek, the way they lean and fall and dance
or don't. I drift with the flow, not like a salmon
swimming against the rage but downstream through rapids
and pools and sometimes resting on the bank.
It's always been this way, as a child I called the corners
of my bed the names of movie theaters
and when I closed my eyes, the show began.
A movie is an illness suffering hot and cold sweats,
so embrace, I say, the all-mighty Cynic's math:
dump the outtakes, finish the film and start another.
There is no end, no beginning, only a passion
for art and life, those twins coiled in the nest.

The Idiot-Savant Says

I'm such a liar: A Fellini Lexicon is a book based on two interviews conducted by Damian Pettigrew in the summers of 1991 and 1992, a year before Fellini's death. Each interview lasted eight hours and was filmed using three Betacam SP cameras.

Fellini, the director of *La Strada, La Dolce Vita, 8 ½, Amarcord,* and twenty other films, was famous for telling tall tales about his life and work; in the two interviews with

Pettigrew he admitted as much. Take, for instance, the meaning of Amarcord. In one place he says the movie was named after a Swedish abortionist named Hammercord. In another, that it is a amalgam of *amare,* to love, *core*, heart, *ricordare* to remember and *amaro* bitter.

He said that for the first two days he directs the movie, then the movie directs him. He follows an idea wherever it leads. Dying is an incentive to finish a film and start another. In the spirit of perversity that characterized him, I have lifted some of the things he said in the interviews and cobbled them together into a poem. I know he forgives me, for he said that the clock is death, but the creativity clock conquers death.

Easter

They were thought
to be miracle or monsters,
    of the Lord
  or from the devil.
You changed that when you looked
  and etched them onto copper
    exact
  with feeling
captives in cocoons
  from egg to larvae,
from pupa to the winged adult,
molting, hatching and their floral food.
    They did not rise
    from mud or sin
    but rose
  transformed and winged
  for every day is Easter
    in their world.
  Rising in a flight
life soars from life.

Easter

Maria Sibylla Merian was a German naturalist who observed insects closely and was one of the first artists to draw them in accurate details. At age thirteen she collected them and was particularly fascinated by silkworms, butterflies and moths. She published her first book of illustrations in 1675, and over four years, 1679-1683, she published a two-volume series on 186 species of European insects and their plant hosts, with over a hundred plates engraved by her. The books documented the process of metamorphosis.

> Lord, who createdst man in wealth and store,
>   Though foolishly he lost the same,
>   Decaying more and more,
>   Till he became
>   Most poore:
>   With thee
>   O let me rise
>   As larks, harmoniously,
>   And sing this day thy victories:
> Then shall the fall further the flight in me.
>
> My tender age in sorrow did beginne
>   And still with sicknesses and shame.
>   Thou didst so punish sinne,
>   That I became
>   Most thinne.
>   With thee
>   Let me combine,
>   And feel thy victorie:
>   For, if I imp my wing on thine,
> Affliction shall advance the flight in me.
>   George Herbert

The Day Dawned Bright

Death Of Gilgamesh

Gilgamesh (the) son of Nissum
his beloved wife his son
The wife, his beloved concubine
his musicians beloved chief valet
the palace attendants
        I have seen
           weeps over (it)
        I have seen
           eats bread
        I have seen
           drinks water
like that of a god
    he enters the palace
        hast thou seen
    like a beautiful standard
Him who fell down from the mast
    the pegs pulled out
Him who died a sudden death
    hast thou seen
He lies upon the night couch and drinks pure water
he who was killed in battle
    corpse down the river
His spirit finds no
    rest in the underworld
Gilgamesh (the) son of Nissum
    made heavy
Gilgamesh
which he interpreted to them
    they answer
why dost thy cry?

>   Why has it been made?
> he brought forth
>   there is not
> strength, firm muscle
> escaped not the hand
>   looked upon
>   the
>   seized.

Death Of Gilgamesh

The Gilgamesh stories, which we have in various languages, are the product of the Mesopotamian culture that existed in the plains fed by the Tigris and Euphrates rivers. They are part adventure story and part morality play. Death is a vivid figure throughout.

We have the epic only in fragments on stone tablets. My translation is taken from the word by word translation by E. A. Speiser.

Hot Day In August

What's not widely known:
we were partners in the hunt,
she ranged swiftly far afield
and I followed with the hounds.

It was a hot and sultry day
and thinking I lagged way behind
she lay her quiver, dress and undergarment
on the bank and slipped into a pond.

Tracer, Racer, Quicklight, Blackcoat,
– they caught her scent
and raced merrily to find her.
You know the rest.
I saw
       a girl
           a goddess
                white as moonlight

Wingfoot, Shaggy, Hardhead,
the entire pack looked at me funny.
I was changing, unbelieving.
I took off, heading for the trees
but they, old hounds and young
trained carefully by me for bear and boar,
with sharp barks gained on me ...

       later, the moon rose ...

Hot Day In August

While he hesitates his dogs catch sight of him. First '*Black-foot*', Melampus, and keen-scented Ichnobates, '*Tracker*', signal him with baying, Ichnobates out of Crete, Melampus, Sparta. Then others rush at him swift as the wind, *'Greedy'*, Pamphagus, Dorceus, *'Gazelle'*, Oribasos, *'Mountaineer'*, all out of Arcady: powerful *'Deerslayer'*, Nebrophonos, savage Theron, *'Whirlwind'*, and Laelape, *unter'*. Then swift-footed Pterelas, *'Wings'*, and trail-scenting Agre, *'Chaser'*, fierce Hylaeus, *'Woody'*, lately gored by a boar, the wolf-born Nape, *'Valley'*, Poemenis, the trusty *'Shepherd'*, and Harpyia, *'Snatcher'*, with her two pups. There is thin-flanked Sicyonian Ladon, *'Catcher'*, Dromas, *'Runner'*, *'Grinder'*, Canache, Sticte *'Spot'*, Tigris *'Tigress'*, Alce, *'Strong'*, and white-haired Leucon, *'Whitey'*, and black-haired Asbolus, *'Soot'*. Lacon, *'Spartan'*, follows them, a dog well known for his strength, and strong-running Aëllo, *'Storm'*. Then Thoos, *'Swift'*, and speedy Lycisce, *'Wolf'*, with her brother Cyprius *'Cyprian'*. Next *'Grasper'*, Harpalos, with a distinguishing mark of white, in the centre of his black forehead, *'Black'*, Melaneus, and Lachne, *'Shaggy'*, with hairy pelt, Labros, *'Fury'*, and Argiodus, *'White-tooth'*, born of a Cretan sire and Spartan dam, keen-voiced Hylactor, *'Barker'*, and others there is no need to name. The pack of them, greedy for the prey follow over cliffs and crags, and inaccessible rocks, where the way is hard or there is no way at all. He runs, over the places where he has often chased, flying, alas, from his own hounds. He longs to shout 'I am Actaeon! Know your own master!' but words fail him, the air echoes to the baying.

> Ovid, *Metamorphosis*, from A. S. Kline's Poetry in Translation, a web site of poetry and translation

Daphne Slowed By Mud

She
    standing there white
a sapling stripped of its bark
her face the color of what wildflower?

"How's the weather?"
    she asked and
        bolted from the field
    down the hill
through the village
    past the firehouse
        past the bar
            bounding like a doe

  to the river
where her feet
    were slowed by mud

I caught her
    we were laughing
as we fell into the silt
            together
    once
        and for all time.

Daphne Slowed By Mud

Slowed by mud is a reversal of the myth about Daphne fleeing Apollo. She was a naiad, a female nymph associated with fountains, wells, springs, and streams. Due to a curse on Apollo made by the god Cupid, he was condemned to chase Daphne against her wishes. Just before being kissed by him, Daphne pleaded to her river god father for help, and he transformed her into a laurel tree.

> a heavy numbness seized her limbs, thin bark closed over her breast, her hair turned into leaves, her arms into branches, her feet so swift a moment ago stuck fast in slow-growing roots, her face was lost in the canopy. Only her shining beauty was left.
>
> Even this did not quench Apollo's ardor, and as he embraced the tree, he felt her heart still beating. "My bride," he said, "since you can never be, at least sweet laurel you shall be my tree."

Ovid

The Music Wakes The Foxes

They said I was a god born of a god
but I was young and vain, with spongy bones
cushioned by flesh, ensnared by love and lust.
Then I found an act. The look came first,
curls, a staff, a glass of wine.
My uncle supplied gallons of red
infused with beeswax. And word got around.
They came, the boys and girls, boys
wearing goat pants and girls
with grape vines in their hair.

We start slow, with offerings of figs and apples,
storax and thistles. Then the festive drums and pipes
that dissolve restraint and fear. Our music
wakes the foxes that gather round us.

I lead them in the dance, head thrown back,
eyes glazed, plump hips moving, I slap the air.
They follow, gliding through the almond orchards,
their feet crushing marjoram and thyme,
their tongues thick with delirium.
Throughout the night without eyes,
the music drowned by roars,
they shriek with frenzy, ecstasy and terror.

By dawn they see the light, the slender boys and girls.
Netted and abused, dismembered by their love,
I am a dying god reborn in bliss.

The Music Wakes The Foxes

And as I sat, over the light blue hills
There came a noise of revelers: the rills
Into the wide stream came of purple hue.
Twas Bacchus and his crew!
The earnest trumpet spake, and silver thrills
From kissing cymbals made a merry din.
Twas Bacchus and his kin!
Like to a moving vintage down they came,
Crown'd with green leaves, and faces all on flame;
All madly dancing through the pleasant valley,
To scare thee, Melancholy!
O then, O then, thou wast a simple name!
And I forgot thee, as the berried holly
By shepherds is forgotten, when in June
Tall chestnuts keep away the sun and moon:
I rush'd into the folly!

Within his car, aloft, young Bacchus stood,
Trifling his ivy-dart, in dancing mood,
With sidelong laughing;
And little rills of crimson wine imbrued
His plump white arms and shoulders, enough white
For Venus' pearly bite;
And near him rode Silenus on his ass,
Pelted with flowers as he on did pass
Tipsily quaffing.

          Keats

Frieze Of Girls With Lovely Braids

The day dawned bright and rosy with the slightest breeze.
The maids and I hitched up the mules and drove them
to the washing pools to soak the palace gowns and shirts
and sheets and linen, and to stomp them clean
and spread them out on rocks to dry.
I was an island girl, daughter of the king, sixteen, unwed.

We ate from baskets, drank wine from skins,
then batted back and forth a yellow ball that went flying
to a thicket where our shouts aroused a creature
nearly naked, with a leafy branch to cover
up his maleness. He rose and closed the space between us,
fast, a lion closing on a helpless fawn.
The maids all fled like frightened birds but I,
Nausicaa, stood my ground and faced him.
I wondered if he hurt me, would I beg for mercy,
but it was he who begged:

   o princess, refuge
   a simple seaman   war with Troy
   a witch   and Cyclops
   sea   and shipwrecked
and he called me lovely
   white arms   shiny braids
and other honeyed words.

I took mercy on him, gave him soap
to wash and virgin oil to oil his skin.
He turned aside to scour the sea brine
off his crusted body. I'd never seen a mortal man
so beautiful and large, his shoulders broad,

his hair, now clean, flowing down
his sun-scorched back,
and when he turned around,
his face was gleaming like a god's.

Frieze Of Girls With Lovely Braids

Frieze of girls is taken from Scott Moncrief's mistranslation of a chapter in Proust's *In Search of Time Lost*.

Naturally and in abundance fine bodies with fine legs, fine hips, wholesome and reposeful faces, with an air of agility and guile. And were they not noble and calm models of human beauty that I beheld there, outlined against the sea, like statues exposed to the sunlight upon a Grecian shore?

Proust

Odysseus's behavior in the Nausicaa chapter is so out of character that many people have wondered if Homer wrote it. Robert Graves decided that Nausicaa herself wrote it. He goes further, saying she wrote all of the Odyssey, and it bolsters his idea to note that in recounting his adventures to Penelope, Odysseus doesn't mention Nausicaa.

The Other One

The thick honey flowed so slowly from the bottle
that our hostess had the time to say,
"Here in sad Crimea where we've been brought by fate,
we're never bored.
We celebrate the rites of Bacchus;
the days roll on like heavy barrels.
Go outside, you'll find dark curtains
over windows like lashes over eyes,
you'll encounter dogs and watchmen,
you might hear voices from the huts
but you won't understand them and won't reply.
Walk past the gleaming pillars to the vineyards
that are glowing in the glassy air.
There is all the art and wisdom of Hellenic culture."

We sat in the white room, silence like a spinning wheel.
It smelled of vinegar and paint and wine cool from the cellar.
I thought of her, in the Greek house, the wife,
not Helen, the other one, who kept on weaving
and of him, his ship battered by the heavy waves,
his sails exhausted by the winds,
and how she was bewildered by him
when he approached her filled with space and time.

The Other One

The poem is roughly adapted from Mandelstam. Born to a secular and sophisticated Jewish family, he never felt fully at home in Russia and embraced Western culture and the Greek world of the Black Sea.

Theseus In The Maze
talking to himself

. . . and devious Daedalus, what's his interest in all this?
He built the bull to please that queen,
then the maze to hide her monstrous issue.
"Go forward, ever forward," Ariadne said,
"always down." Her hot string
unwinds without a tangle. Will it snap
and I entombed, a victim of a plot
to leave me wandering
like a Sisyphus of twists and turns?
Or is this dream? I'll hoist a white sail
of surrender and wake in Athens
with my buddies and our girls.

She slipped and called him Asterion,
a star. Does she love the idiot offspring
of a weird obsession? The creature
may be innocent, the maze itself the monster,
a convoluted pit like love without escape.
But there's no choice, whether love or hate,
once on the path to taurine hell
a man must trust love's thread
and go and meet his fate.

Theseus In The Maze

In classical times the Minotaur was depicted as having the head and tail of a bull and the body of a man, in medieval times as having the head and torso of a man and the body of a bull. At his birth the Minotaur was named Asterion, "the starry one," a name that was also given to the King of Crete who preceded Minos. After Theseus killed the Minotaur, he and Ariadne sailed for Athens, but he deserted her on the island of Naxos.

Ariadne's Llament

Waking on the beach, stirring, still sleepy
my hand reached out for you
and there was nothing.
I turned over and reached out
and nothing, no one there.
And moved my arm across where you had been
and groped the empty air.

I ran a little way, my feet dragged
down by heavy sand
and back
and up
the beach, treading in your footprints,
shouting out your name
    Theseus
and the cliff responded in a languid echo
    see-us
as if the place itself cried out for you.

I climbed a hill and it was then
I saw the southern wind stretch the sail.
Wait, I shrieked and waved my arms
thinking you would see me
and realize that you'd left your love behind.
    Wait!
and beat my chest
    Come back!
  the words and blows in rhythm.
I shouted one last time.
The ship sailed on, a shrinking speck

turned into sky, swallowed
by the mild blue vapor.

Now first frost coats the ground like shattered glass,
birds hidden in the trees lament the coming of the chill.
I see no people, cattle, cultivated fields,
                just sea, a sea without a sail.
And if there were a sail, where would I go?
Not back to Crete, to the father I betrayed
or to Athens where I'd find you in the palace
                boasting of your exploits.
You should have killed me with the bull
who was despite your lies a gentle creature.

Now I fear more than I grieve. I fear the serpents
who will sting me and the lions who will tear my flesh.
You left me here to die alone,
for death to scatter first my soul, then my bones.

Ariadne's Lament

Abandoned by Theseus on Naxos, Ariadne is usually portrayed as a victim, but her story is more complicated than that. She was discovered on the beach by Dionysus; they married and had children. Her wedding diadem was set in the sky as the constellation Corona Borealis. Although a goddess, she was mortal. Some myths say Artemis killed her; others that Persius killed her at Argos, still others that she hanged herself from a tree. Given the various accounts of her life and death, it seems she came to represent all women, betrayer, triumphant, betrayed, divine.

In The Great Hall

I was one of the good ones.
I argued against slaying the son, twice!
But when the time came
Ulysses' mouth foamed with fury.

Wait, I cried,
I stumbled on her picking out the weft,
unweaving what she'd woven,
she even showed me how she does it,
yet I said nothing to the others.

He notched an arrow. I raised my sword and rushed him.
It was then his son, the one I'd saved, thrust his spear
into my back between the shoulders with such force
it spurted out my chest. I looked down astonished,
and fell forwa . . .

In The Great Hall

Amphinomus was the nicest of Penelope's suitors and twice dissuaded the others from killing Telemachus. Odysseus told him to leave while the leaving was good but Athena compelled him to stay.

Astarte In Hades

To prepare, three days of fasting,
then a day to wash herself
in a radiant stream,
her hair combed and brushed,
her head crowned with roses
her body clothed in seven robes.
Step by step down
throwing off a robe at every gate
until,
as queen of heaven
she enters hell,
her glowing nakedness abolishing the dark.

Astarte In Hades

My poem is adapted from a stanza by Angelos Sikelianos

A similar poem by Mandelstam

When Life descends, like Persephone, a blind swallow
with a green twig throws herself at her feet.
Phantoms rise to greet her, fugitives
filled with awe and hope, their thin laments
falling like fine rain on leafless trees.
One holds out a mirror, another a phial of perfume.
Life likes things so she takes them.
In confusion what to do she breathes gently on the mirror,
unsure if she is dead or not, and she looks
across the misty river and is slow
to give the boatman his little copper coin.

Priapus's Complaint

Let dogs sleep. Sirius and I
will watch for thieving thieves and birds
and boys and girls who think that night's cloak
will conceal them. In gardens and fields,
I endure hot sun and freezing nights,
my sickle raised against them all.

Neptune's trident, Mars' sword, Hercules his club,
they all display their thing, so I mine
standing tall for all to savor.

As for looks, Apollo has his beauty, Cupid's comely,
but they don't sport what I sport.

Sparrows in the spring, old crows, wet geese,
thirsty ravens and young robins –
so wives and boys and girls flock to me
for something they can't find at home.

Thieves come for fruit and when
I'm done with them they whimper
"must I endure this for a cabbage?"
They come here wanting that
and they get this instead.

But I get lonely in these flower beds
with flowers I can't pluck,
in wide fields I never get to plow.
I get fondled, pricked, poked, rubbed, pawed
but never loved. Although I'm wood
I'm filled with sap. Can't they see
within the wood my hot heart?

Priapus's Complaint

Priapus, in his capacity as garden god, has two duties: to encourage the fecundity of the garden and to act as a scarecrow. He accomplishes both tasks by means of his huge erect phallus. In first century Rome, some poets, perhaps Ovid and Virgil among them, wrote the Priapeia, ninety-five satirical and obscene epigrams on the subject of poor Priapus. Two samples:

> Why the laughter girl?
> Sure I wasn't carved by Praxiteles or Scopas
> but by a farmer from a shapeless log
> who said Thou Art Priapus,
> yet you giggle because you think it droll,
> my thing, my glorious column.

> Acclaimed darling of the clubs, while Quinctia rattles
> her cymbals, thumps her tambourine
> and lowers her rump to the floor,
> she is secretly praying that her mob
> of admirers are standing as tall as Priapus.

The Hour Is Getting Late

Branch Bent Down With Snow

In this early retirement of wits
forgetting words and losing keys
urine dribbling down my pant leg
watching tired TV thrillers
eating a whole packet
that's been invaded by mice
as for print, it's too tiny

Sitting in an outdoor café
listening to ice falling in the ice machine
and the faucet dripping into the cat's dish
I stopped and took _____?
Strange, I know the word
it's there, the word.
I took
a moment?
Notice?
Advantage of the moment?
Took *stock* in the warehouse of lost words
and fading memories

Spring – a lover who comes and goes
and me with liver spots and drooling.
Sadness is as unpredictable as mornings
(both the deep kind and the pleasant).
Two swallows making love
and spring is just an old fool

This cruel year has deflected me
like a river from its course.
My life has flowed into a sister channel

of shallow waters filled with vapors
and vipers and tree stumps.

I sang
   eternal love
     of clouds and sky
this dream of me
        "Jim Levy"
for a long time foolish
then a flood of words
now astonished to be here still

Speak to me mirror
no sarcasm now no evasions
who's that bag of being?
Whose face is that with mother
and father assembled,
her drinks his women?
I forgive them and the future
and this is what is strange
they forgive me

So I ask my doctor
   and he cites the I Ching
the body he says is a rag in the corner
and the heart, it's just doing its job
   and has no answers

My friends they agree
any time now is all the time
because for old men everything
is too much or too little

wine can't slake our thirst
women should speak more quietly
the slightest tear is a gash

We thought we were outward bound
but the sun is coming for us
we were the center of the universe
and now charred specks

There's a strange crater in my chest
a lull in the clash
between boredom and love
When the voice of reason intercedes
I step outside and walk under a branch
bent down with snow

You're old and I want to know
what does that feel like please
is it like floating in the Salton Sea?
  yes
and you have to be old to understand that
  yes
and you cherish it
  it's not an it it's a feeling
  a feeling that feels like nothing
I don't understand
  that's the point

and this is connected to your mother
  yes
she felt and didn't understand
  yes

didn't understand that you didn't want her to suffer
>   *yes*
your children, do they know you lived
>   *yes they know*

It's becoming my coffin
this room
walls lined with books
a felt hat hanging on a nail
and between two blue curtains
the pale light of evening

I'm tired of looking out
there's nothing out there
>   and I can't see it
the message is excess
my exile a mistake.

Branch Bent Down With Snow

>   This cruel age has deflected me,
>   like a river from this course.
>   Strayed from its familiar shores,
>   my changeling life has flowed
>   into a sister channel.
>   How many spectacles I've missed:
>   the curtain rising without me,
>   and falling too. How many friends
>   I never had the chance to meet.
>   Akhmatova

And I Said, Oh Place

Does the blackened ruin in the stony ground between Durraj
and Mutathallam
belong to the tribe of Ummi Awfa? If so, why, when I address it,
doesn't it speak to me? Wasn't this their dwelling in the grassy
meadows
where wild cows wandered, their young springing up at birth?

I stood again by their encampment – it's been twenty years –
and knew it slowly, recognized three stones blackened
by the fires where kettles used to hang. And I said, oh place,
good morning, have you been safe from danger?

And I saw women traveling on camels, covering the high
ground
above the stream of Jurthum. They had sheltered their howdahs
with cloth of high value, with tassels of red like dripping blood.

And I Said, Oh Place

Zuhayr bin Abī Sūlmā was one of the premier poets who lived in sixth century Arabia before the coming of Muhammad. His poems can be found in Hammad Ar-Rawiya's anthology, the Mu'allaqat ("the Suspended"), a collection of pre-Islamic poetry. He was one of the Seven Hanged Poets who were reputed to have been honored by hanging copies of their work in the Kaaba at Mecca.

My poem is an excerpt from his long poem about a forty-year-old feud between two tribes and how it was stopped by two nobles, but was then started again by another man who still sought revenge. The poem concludes with Zuhayr's acidic view of life and some wise sayings.

Rilke In Ronda

On December 9, 1912, five days after his thirty-seventh birthday, Rilke arrived in Ronda, an ancient town in the mountains of Andalusia. Toward the end of his stay, having returned from a long walk in the mountains, he sat on the terrace of his hotel and wrote a letter to his friend and patron, Princess Marie von Thurn und Taxis-Hohenlohe.

At last Princess,
I have found a refuge for my wretched desolation,
a place of sky and silence, stone and solitude.
To be here is *to be here,* to seek the vein of ore
that travels through the hardest stone,
to stand amazed before the deep abyss
of layered air, to gaze upward at a sky
so deeply blue that would, if it descended, crush us.

At first I thought it a mistake to come here
hoping to be transformed. I still had Venice in me,
bored with women who were shooting stars
of burning dust, bored with looking but not seeing,
seeing but not being, and bored with death,
that darkness in my heart.
Venice, where I sought a reclamation
of my spirit and – nothing happened.
For yea I say with Saint Angela that if the saints
and god himself console but do not enter me
and change me, then they merely vex
my grief and rage and blindness.

One day I found a park, a snake
was hissing at a hawk, and lesser kestrels

scored the sky. I sat and read your letter.
Princess, your letter! Coming just in time to ask me,
if I had a home would I go home, and to question
if I have a void where two sides of existence,
mind and body, meet. You remind me that I
worship . . . no, I leave for Paris soon
and will tell you when we meet.

Another walk, through oak trees to the meadows
that surround the town, an encounter
with a shepherd brown from years of sun,
slow of step but quick to sling his stones
to keep his flock hemmed in,
a man not fleeing his existence.
He links me to the human which
turns toward me and with a simple gesture
knows me, grasps me.

Clouds obscure the sun, a bleak wind rises,
I hurry back to tea the way the English serve it
and this terrace and this letter,
where I gaze and gaze upon the mountains
and show them to myself, the gaze that penetrates
and pierces me and is returned as world-as-language,
these mountains floating in the purest air.

Spring is near. The Spanish fig tree's sap
has risen, then the flowers. Then the fruit!
Art is all. The rest is dust.
Images and sounds flow through the poem
as through a prism, reflected and dispersed,
and proclaim their affinity to music.
The miracle has happened.

I participate in what exists. Angels sing but we –
we sing and are and then are changed,
and between the twists of fate and blows of choice,
we praise, and I become at last a finished voice.

Rilke In Ronda

Ronda, in the mountains sixty miles northwest of Málaga, consists of two towns, each perched on rock separated by El Tajo, the deep gorge of the Rio Guadalévin. Rilke was in Ronda for nine and a half weeks, from mid-December 1912 to the third week of February. He stayed at the Hotel Reina Victoria, a hotel with a decaying grandeur although it was less than ten years old. It was run by a Quaker lady and catered to British tourists and military families from Gibraltar but was nearly empty in the winter. He was given room 208 with a view of la Serrania de Ronda, the limestone mountains of stony outcrops and fir trees that surround Ronda.

When he arrived in Ronda Rilke was suffering from the angst that characterized much of his life, but within weeks he was writing poetry again and had regained his sense of purpose. He continued the *Duino Elegies*, beginning the sixth and adding to the ninth, and completed the poems called *The Spanish Trilogy*, *Experience* and *Lazarus*.

Ronda contains several reminders of the poet, including a bronze statue of him gazing into the gorge and a short Avenida Poeta Rilke. The Hotel Reina Victoria still exists but has been transformed into an elegant boutique hotel. For many years, room 208 was a museum containing Rilke's writing stand and other mementos, but when the hotel was remodeled, the museum was closed and a few of his things were put in a glass display case just off the bar.

It contains a photo of the poet, a couple of books, a framed page in his handwriting, and a faded copy of his hotel bill.

Me Gusta la Vida Enormemente
César Vallejo

César, I too like life enormously,
train stations with wooden benches,
and yes, cafés and the viola with its rare sound,
the bare flesh of trout fillets with a rough white
and the gongs of buoys in weather.

Do we like it enough to sweeten our words
with the fragrance of lemon grass,
to wander down streets with clocks on every corner?
But that was a dream and a dream is life too.

And like you I like it on my own terms,
possessing what possesses me,
the children's wild thinking and poems by Dario.

There have been times, liking life,
I've lived like a fool,
swimming in the drink and loving
a woman with glossy brown hair.

So yes, I like life enormously
because when we love we love everything.

Me Gusta la Vida Enormemente

My poem was inspired by Vallejo's poem about liking life enormously but he didn't like life enormously; he didn't like it at all. It's true that in the middle of the poem, he writes *Me gusta la vida enormemente* but the poem begins *Hoy me gusta la vida mucho menos,* Today I like life much less, and then he says

    I like life enormously,

>   but of course
>   with my beloved death and my café
>   and looking at the leafy chestnut trees of Paris . . .
>   so much life and never!

I liked life enormously up to age forty-six, when I lost the sight in one eye and some sight in the other. At least that's what I tell myself. But I started writing dark poems at age twenty and part of me became melancholy even earlier, around age twelve. It may have been simply a recognition of mortality, mine and everyone's, which is enough to make anyone a poet. In Vallejo's case, it may have been his birth without sufficient oxygen at 10,240 feet in a remote town in northern Peru or, as some have suggested, it may have been a product of his stoic Indian ancestry, but if there's one poet who did not suffer stoically it is Vallejo. Still another theory, mine, is that he was at birth (the eleventh and final child) torn between powerful traditions; both his grandmothers were Chimu Indians and both his grandfathers were Catholic priests.

Comprenderán Todos Los Hombres
César Vallejo

All men will understand, but Vallejo,
I don't understand your poetry
   but I do
I don't understand when you say
how little has died this afternoon
   but I have
and in Spain, when you say
a book sprouts from the corpse
you raise grief to an absolute.

It's hard for me to comprehend
your charmed life full of agony,
years rowing with one oar
feeling the sun on the side of your face,
parking your bony chest on a bench in Paris
and how, after the rain, clouds appear in the puddles.

It's true you do explain a few things
such as there are pebbles embedded in the path
and splinters in the flesh,
but what do you mean when you say
you have sorrow in one eye and sorrow in the other?
Sure we're beaten with sticks for no reason
and after some history, we die,
but there can be too much compassion, too much pity.
It's time we abandon our poor occupation of space
because I do understand that the corpse goes on dying.

Comprenderán Todos Los Hombres

In a poem written in 1974, Charles Bukowski (not a poet himself, just an attitude flouted in thirty-five books) wrote:

> it is hard to find a man
> whose lines do not
> turn against you.
> Vallejo never offended.

César Abraham Vallejo Mendoza never offended? He offended relentlessly, usually intentionally. He was at times sentimental, vulgar, bitter, incoherent, bathetic, aggressive and passive-aggressive. Of his Andes, he wrote: *Condors? Screw the condors!* Although he had an immense compassion for his parents and for humanity at large, he didn't have much for individuals or for himself. Yet, and this yet is why poets and lovers of poetry worship him, he expressed in the most anguished, raw and eloquent way the pathos of the human condition.

Vallejo worked in a mine and a sugar plantation, but he also attended several universities in Lima and nearer to home, in Trujillo, and received a bachelor degree. He published his first poem at age nineteen and studied law for nearly three years. After several disastrous love affairs, he shot himself but survived. At age twenty-eight, he was indicted for participating in the burning down of a store and the subsequent death of two policemen, a charge that may have been justified. Out on bail for two years, which he spent as a teacher, he fled to Paris when legal proceedings were reopened. He lived in Paris for the next fifteen years, except for visits to Russia, two tours of European cities and two years in Spain. He died age forty-eight in Paris of unknown cause.

Maktub

Maktub appears once in the Quran, at 7:157, where it states that the coming of Muhammad is anticipated in the Torah and Gospels. The word meant written or decreed but it has come to mean that everything is predetermined.

Everything that happens is determined by the stars
or genes or by He who inks on us our fates.
But if He knows already, does He care?
Does He smile to see his work?
There's so much casual evil in the world.

Behind its bars of rage, the caged bird
sings of freedom. The stars don't speak,
genes shrink with age. When His hand slips
the diamond's sold as dust.

Maktub

> A free bird leaps
> on the back of the wind
> and floats downstream
> till the current ends
> and dips his wing
> in the orange sun rays
> and dares to claim the sky.
> But a bird that stalks
> down his narrow cage
> can seldom see through
> his bars of rage
> his wings are clipped and
> his feet are tied

so he opens his throat to sing.
The caged bird sings
with a fearful trill
of things unknown
but longed for still
and his tune is heard
on the distant hill
for the caged bird
sings of freedom.
The free bird thinks of another breeze
and the trade winds soft through the sighing trees
and the fat worms waiting on a dawn bright lawn
and he names the sky his own
But a caged bird stands on the grave of dreams
his shadow shouts on a nightmare scream
his wings are clipped and his feet are tied
so he opens his throat to sing.
The caged bird sings
with a fearful trill
of things unknown
but longed for still
and his tune is heard
on the distant hill
for the caged bird
sings of freedom.
     Angelou

I met a traveler from an antique land,
Who said – "Two vast and trunkless legs of stone
Stand in the desert. . . . Near them, on the sand,
Half sunk a shattered visage lies, whose frown,

And wrinkled lip, and sneer of cold command,
Tell that its sculptor well those passions read
Which yet survive, stamped on these lifeless things,
The hand that mocked them, and the heart that fed;
And on the pedestal, these words appear:
My name is Ozymandias, King of Kings;
Look on my Works, ye Mighty, and despair!
Nothing beside remains. Round the decay
Of that colossal Wreck, boundless and bare
The lone and level sands stretch far away.
      Shelley

Tyger Tyger, burning bright,
In the forests of the night;
What immortal hand or eye,
Could frame thy fearful symmetry?

In what distant deeps or skies
Burnt the fire of thine eyes?
On what wings dare he aspire?
What the hand, dare seize the fire?

And what shoulder, & what art,
Could twist the sinews of thy heart?
And when thy heart began to beat,
What dread hand? & what dread feet?

What the hammer? what the chain,
In what furnace was thy brain?
What the anvil? what dread grasp,
Dare its deadly terrors clasp!

When the stars threw down their spears
And water'd heaven with their tears:
Did he smile his work to see?
Did he who made the Lamb make thee?

Tyger Tyger burning bright,
In the forests of the night:
What immortal hand or eye,
Dare frame thy fearful symmetry?
                              Blake

Even When It's Dark
After Mayakovsky

Spring became July and it was so hot
every day as the sun burned down on us
and the nights were hot too

I yelled at the sun wait don't go
   come have a drink
because I still loved the sun then
every day I whispered don't go

and the sun rolled up the valley
like a tire come off a milk truck
and up the hill across the yard
to the door and didn't knock
but burst right in
the whole being golden

I tried to hide my fear
and said sit down
   have some tea and toast
   some jam a rum and coke
the heat was tremendous
it filled the room
sweat ran down my back
as we sank down on the greasy couch
and talked
   Levy the sun said Listen
   I shine all the time
   even when it's dark

We sat on the couch
remembering together the days
we spent in the soft hills
me well-built newly married
removing my clothes
and spreading out on a hilltop
first my back and buttocks
becoming red
then my face and chest
in an act of worship

We talked until dark
and there was no dark
everywhere
and in the end the sun said
   then it's agreed we'll shine
   all day and night me as usual
   and you in verse.

Even When It's Dark

Poet, staunch Bolshevik, melancholy lover, Vladimir Vladimirovich Mayakovsky was the most revered Soviet poet of his day, until he was not. Tall, over 6'2, a madcap, he was part Beat, part Abbie Hoffman, with an undercoat of despair. His father was a Cossack, his mother Ukrainian and his first language was Georgian, yet he embraced socialism and then communism with entirely Russian excess. At age 36, a bullet pierced his heart. Either he shot himself out of despair over his complex love life or his treatment by Stalin's surrogates, or he was murdered. The debate continues to this day.

A hundred and forty suns
and summer rolled into July;
it was so hot,
the heat blazed in a haze
and this was in the country.
And next morning,
to flood the world again,
the sun rose red.

Day after day
I shouted at the sun:
"Stop!
Stop sinking into the abyss.
At the sun I yelled:
"You shiftless pile of light!
You're caressed by the clouds,
while here, winter and summer
I sit and draw these posters!"
I yelled at the sun again:
"Hold on!
Listen, goldbrow,
instead of going down,
why not come have tea
with me!"

O man what did I do?
Now I'm for it.
Toward me, in his own good time,
spreading his beams,
the sun strode across the field.
I tried to hide my fear,
and beat it down.

His eyes were in the garden
and then he came to the house
pressing through the windows,
doors, and crannies;
and in he rolled

and the sun says:
calm down, don't worry,
look at things honestly.
Do you think
I find it easy
to shine?
Just try it.
You'll move along,
since move you must;
you'll move and shine your eyes out!"

We gossiped until dark,
except there was no darkness here.
We warmed up to each other
and soon, in friendship,
I slapped him on the back.
The sun responded!
"You and I,
my comrade, are quite a pair!
Let's go, my poet,
let's shine and sing
in this dreary worn-out world.
I shall pour forth my light
and you – your own,
in verse."
    Excerpts from the Mayakovsky poem

Then will we chide the sun for letting night
    Take up his place and right:
We sing one common Lord; wherefore he should
    Himself the candle hold.
I will go searching, till I find a sun
    Shall stay, till we have done;
A willing shiner, that shall shine as gladly,
    As frost-nipped suns look sadly.
Then will we sing, and shine all our own day,
    And one another pay:
His beams shall cheer my breast, and both so twine,
Till ev'n His beams sing, and my music shine.

George Herbert

Drape The Day In Precious Linen

Born a Levite, I was not raised one
   but still, my childhood – one of sorrow
My mother – sorrow   My father, often absent – sorrow.
When I taste an olive, I taste sorrow
    hearing songs I sorrow
sunlight is infected with it
              even love is drenched in sorrow.

Born a Levite, I was not raised one
  but with the priests,
waiting with them by the river
I kept the morning watch.
     When the sky turned yellow
I did behold the clarity of dawn, the light.
   So when and why did I inhale
           these fumes of non-existence?

Drape The Day In Precious Linen

    A young Levite among the priests
    keeps the morning watch
    as the Jewish night thickens around them
    and the temple falls into ruin.
    He feels threatened by the yellow sky.
    Run, Jews, night envelopes the Euphrates.
    But the priests think, this is not our fault.
    Behold the black and yellow light, the joy, the Jews.
    For he was with us on the river's bank
    when we draped the holy day in precious linen
    and lit the city's night and inhaled the fumes of
    nothingness.

                              Mandelstam

Poet, lover, runner and all-round athlete
and as beautiful as Endymion,
his family not unfamiliar with the Synagogue,
he said:
"The days I most value are the ones
when I relinquish art and the pursuit of
perfect and perishable white limbs,
and I become what I was born to be:
of the Jews, son of the holy Jews."

"of the Jews, son of the . . ."
Somewhat excessive, that declaration.
He didn't become one, not even close.
Hedonism and art claimed him, that boy.
                                    Cavafy

What Of The Night

Set me on the watchtower, to stand upon the watch
and cry Why
How long Lord
will the women cry out
and the children cry out of violence

Set me upon the tower to watch
for bitter horsemen from the east
They do not tarry
and will surely come
and You are not near

The shriek of locust on the land
the tocsin ringing
the wail of our lament
and You do not hear

What are we
what is our life
what is our goodness

Woe to them
who don't t accept their fate
grain separated from the chaff
earth soaked in earth.

I looked Lord
and found parched clay and ravens
watched and waited
for the hasty riders from the east

Stand upon the watch
set me upon the tower
Lord.

What Of The Night

When the valley of Arroyo Hondo was settled in 1815, the Governor of New Mexico degreed in the land grant that the farmers had to be armed. The people of Taos, ten miles to the south, didn't want to have to rush to the settlers' rescue when Ute, Navajo or Comanches came for women, children and livestock. The settlers built two watchtowers, called *atalayas*, at either end of the valley to use as lookouts for raiders.

Prepare the table, watch in the watchtower, eat, drink: arise, ye princes, and anoint the shield.
For thus hath the Lord said unto me, Go, set a watchman, let him declare what he seeth.
And he saw a chariot with a couple of horsemen, a chariot of asses, and a chariot of camels; and he hearkened diligently with much heed:

And he cried, A lion: My lord, I stand continually upon the watchtower in the daytime, and I am set in my ward whole nights:

And, behold, here cometh a chariot of men, with a couple of horsemen. And he answered and said, Babylon is fallen, is fallen; and all the graven images of her gods he hath broken unto the ground.

O my threshing, and the corn of my floor: that which I have heard of the LORD of hosts, the God of Israel, have I declared unto you.

Watchman, what of the night? Watchman, what of the night?

Isaiah

There are many here among us who feel that life is but

a joke
But you and I, we've been through that, and this is not our fate
So let us not talk falsely now, the hour is getting late

All along the watchtower, princes kept the view
While all the women came and went, barefoot servants, too

Outside in the distance a wildcat did growl
Two riders were approaching, the wind began to howl.

Bob Dylan

She Must Have Been Large

Pavese, you are with them aren't you, the girls
who cut through the woods to the beach
and sit at dusk around a fire telling stories
about how the seaweed clings to their bare flesh
and drags them down and how the shadows on the seabed
grow huge. There are eyes down there,
at the bottom of the sea, that gleam.
The girls are fresh and smell good and the sea is calm
and the air is warm. You ask them, would any girl
dare swim at night, alone and naked, like that foreign woman
who did every night and didn't return.
She must have been large
and very white for the eyes to have seen her.

And you are with that old man who rises from his hollow
in the sand when the sea is still dark
and lights a fire from driftwood. The sand grows hot
and he thinks that soon the sea will be blazing too.
Deaf, he can't hear the soft splashing of the waves.
A pale greenish star is surprised by the dawn
and he wants to go back to sleep,
he wants to silence once and for all the silence.

She Must Have Been Large

Cesare Pavese, Italian poet, novelist, translator and essayist, received the Strega Prize, Italy's most prestigious literary award, in June of 1950. He said to a friend, "The trouble with these things is that they always come when one is already through with them and running after strange, different gods." The gods he chased were love and death.

Love was unattainable. Two months after winning the Strega, he took sleeping pills and left a note. "I forgive everyone and ask everyone's forgiveness. Okay? Don't gossip too much."

They'll Meet In Heaven, Stars

Was Horace joking when he called to men of sense
to forsake Rome and settle blessed islands
where virgin soil is fruitful, figs and melon thrive,
there's harvests every year, goats come willingly
for milking and streams leap like laughing feet?

Marvell takes the hint, his sailors sail to remote Bermuda
where they land upon a grassy shore
safe from storm and prelate's rage.
The weather's always spring and winds are songs,
the fruit: bright oranges hanging lanterns in a green night.

And Donne while flat in sickness on his bed
thinks himself a map, calls his ship his ark
and any sea that swallows him his blood.
He imagines passing through the straits
in rapture to see his West
or sailing East to eastern riches and Jerusalem:
on a map east and west are one,
and so, being Donne, he says that death
is one with resurrection.

Campion's weather-beaten sailor longs for shore
and final rest, flees the storm to port
crying " O come quickly, sweetest Lord,
and take my soul to rest."

But poor Drummond's honest fisher
doesn't need greedy Charon or his skiff,
he has his own and dies at sea, his boat his bier.

While Henry King denies the truth.
He pictures ship and tide taking him
to join his Anne dead at twenty-four

and Lovelace too won't let blue-eyed Neptune
separate him from *his* true love:
they'll meet in heaven, stars,
and greet as angels greet.

These poets sailed on maps, not seas
using rhyme as sails and beats as oars
and so their verse soared to fancied heights.
But every sailor knows that storms
reveal the face of God and His intent,
and reaching shore they end as blackened
sea-soaked bodies on the shining sands.

They'll Meet In Heaven, Stars

> Our age, ravaged by civil war
> and Rome itself is collapsing under
> its own weight.
> My advice – sail to some island
> where the fields are fertile,
> rich with grain, and vines flower
> by themselves, and figs and olives
> thrive. I tell you honey drips from trees
> and goats come on their own accord
> for milking, sheep too to be shorn.
> Furthermore there's no bears in the sheepfold
> or snakes in the vineyards.
> You'd be happy there,
> and filled with wonder.
>
> Horace

Whilst my physicians by their love are grown
        Cosmographers, and I their map, who lie
Flat on this bed, that by them may be shown
        That this is my south-west discovery,
    Per fretum febris, by these straits to die,

I joy, that in these straits I see my west;
        For, though their currents yield return to none,
What shall my west hurt me? As west and east
        In all flat maps (and I am one) are one,
    So death doth touch the resurrection.

Is the Pacific Sea my home? Or are
        The eastern riches? Is Jerusalem?
Anyan, and Magellan, and Gibraltar,
        All straits, and none but straits, are ways to them,
    Whether where Japhet dwelt, or Cham, or Shem.

                                      Donne

Death In Venice (Calif)

I wake to warm air on my skin
and always the surf, the booming runs
along the falling wave, subsiding to silence.
When the sun comes out the sea turns green
and sunlight sparkles on the wet sand.
Two white stormbirds cross the sky.

        thump thump thump
a chopper overhead on the lookout for gangs
finds an old man in a chair bronzing his body
and a large Jamaican woman sing-songing
up and down the beach
selling slices of melon and mangos
and two young men on towels rubbing lotion on each other
and comical the seagull with a white neck and black eye
looking for a snatch strutting back and forth like a hooker
but mostly a young woman in a red bikini standing
in a few feet of water gazing out to sea,
then splashing water on herself and laughing.

I waded in and she was friendly and attractive,
a Puerto Rican down from San Francisco
for the warmer water,
can't swim out because she has a broken collarbone,
me, I say I'm from New Mexico and this may be
the last time I see the ocean.
    Why?
    I'm 78.
    No!
    Yes, and at my age, it could happen any time
this in surging water up to our thighs.

Death In Venice (Calif)

He had been young and crude with the times and had taken false steps, blundered, exposed, offending in speech and in writing against tact and good sense.

... he asked his sober, weary heart if a new enthusiasm, a new preoccupation, some late adventure of the feelings could still be in store for him, the idle traveler.

... then he dragged a reclining chair through the pale yellow sand, closer to the sea, sat down, and composed himself.

Little crisping shivers ran all across the wide stretch of shallow water between the shore and the first sand bank. The whole beach, once so full of color and life, looked now autumnal. It was nearly deserted, and not even very clean. A camera on a tripod stood at the edge of the water, apparently abandoned; its black cloth snapping in the freshening wind.

Some minutes passed before anyone hastened to the aid of the elderly man sitting there collapsed in his chair.

Thomas Mann

Isle Full Of Sweet Airs

There the glassy green sea
and pale blue sky are horizontal.
After a hot day the bars stay open all night.
A long dock of gray almost white planks
inserts itself into the sea,
and at the end, standing,
a daughter of the Caribbean,
a dark-skinned girl in a pink bikini.

Isle Full Of Sweet Airs

>My child my sister
>think how sweet it would be
>living there, loving
>and living and dying there
>in the land that mirrors you.
>
>The charm of mysteries there,
>of your eyes shining through your tears
>like misty sunlight
>
>where all is order, beauty,
>luxury and calm.
>
>In our room, deep mirrors reflect
>gleaming furniture, flowers mix their perfumes
>with the scent of amber, the splendor
>whispers to us in its own soft native tongue
>
>while all is order, beauty,
>rich, serene, and calm.
>
>   Baudelaire

A Word Then

Do we understand the deathness in all things?
Do we have to choose between the forgetfulness
that gets forgotten or a willed demise?
Life ends slowly with white mold on the orange
or suddenly under rubble.
We leave like an intruder with nothing
wondering if there is an enormous hand
guiding the ship, an order
we don't recognize as order
or is all shipwreck on the rocks in dying light.

I don't remember where it was
I first heard the sea at night,
Santa Monica on a summer night
or south of Anzio by the Tyrrhenian Sea
but at the end of a long journey
that's all that's left,
its speaking in tongues of living and dying
and me singing with the waves.

A Word Then

     (for I will conquer it)
     The word final, superior to all,
     Subtle, sent up—what is it?—I listen;
     Are you whispering it, and have been
     all the time, you sea waves?
     Whereto answering , the sea
     Delaying not, hurrying not,
     Whisper'd to me through the night,

and very plainly before daybreak; lisp'd to me
the low and delicious word death.
                              Whitman

On many nights I heard the sound of the sea
and now again the sea running up the polished sand
and back like voices in the distance.
And the clamor of the gulls driven by April
from the walls to the plain, their cries
like ours that echo the avid murmur of the sea
                              Quasimodo

I, Diogo Cão, a navigator,
left this pillar by the swarthy strand
and sailed onward.
Was it worth doing?
Everything is worth doing
when the soul is not small.
Whoever would go beyond the Cape
must go beyond sorrow.
God placed danger and the abyss in the sea
but he also made it heaven's mirror.
                              Pessoa

I'm like a cat crushed by a truck's tires
and burned alive and hanged by boys in a fig tree
but with eight of its lives left
or like a snake crushed to a bloody pulp
or a half-eaten eel

I'm like Belmondo at the wheel of his Alfa Romeo
who living within the logic of the narcissistic montage

detaches himself from time and inserts into it himself
in images that have nothing to do
with the boredom of the hours
or with the slow resplendent death of the afternoon.

As for the future, listen:
your fascist sons will sail on
but I'll stay behind like someone
dreaming of his own downfall
among ruins of ancient civilizations
on seashores where life begins again,
Ravenna or Ostia or Bombay,
it makes no difference,
I shall begin to slowly decompose
in the tormented light of the sea,
a poet, a citizen, forgotten.
                              Pasolini

The Poet

The poet who sits down with a blank page
is empty, devoid of thought, without a clue.
The poem is in the past behind the wall
or waiting for her on the path ahead
or is ripening, within.
She leaves her bed, leaves the room,
leaves the world into the void she fills with words.
Anything can spark: a loom, a sprig
of baby's breath, an abstraction ripe with voice,
green soap or silk or wool,
anything that makes her wonder
and mix lies and truths, amuse, bewilder.
The poem, when it arrives, is not an artifact.
It is a way of being.

The Poet

I was writing a poem about Fellini and what inspires him to start a film and this poem sprang into existence as if with a will of its own.

Like A Jeweler

who fashions lilies our of pearls,
roses out of rubies, violets from amethysts,
and hides them in her safe, (they're not for sale),
the artist makes her art for future ages,
not the market, and conceals within it
what is temporal or lasting.

The jeweler's joy is making something beautiful
out of something beautiful, something
beyond fashion, for fashion passes.
The artist knows that even art
does not prevail, yet she persists.
Her art may age faster than a showgirl
but that is not the point. The point
is making it with passion.

Either way, we know that all things
have a half-life, burn at rates that nature dictates.
Time assails them and they fade, for even passion,
even art, ends in ashes.

Like A Jeweler

The art of losing isn't hard to master;
so many things seem filled with the intent
to be lost that their loss is no disaster.

Lose something every day. Accept the fluster
of lost door keys, the hour badly spent.
The art of losing isn't hard to master.

Then practice losing farther, losing faster:
places, and names, and where it was you meant
to travel. None of these will bring disaster.

I lost my mother's watch. And look! my last, or
next-to-last, of three loved houses went.
The art of losing isn't hard to master.

I lost two cities, lovely ones. And, vaster,
some realms I owned, two rivers, a continent.
I miss them, but it wasn't a disaster.

—Even losing you (the joking voice, a gesture
I love) I shan't have lied. It's evident
the art of losing's not too hard to master
though it may look like (*Write* it!) like disaster.

Elizabeth Bishop

Best Poem Ever 2

Although the thought is tedious
and the poem reads like a weak translation,
I'll tell a story this time, paint a portrait,
say how cold affects the old
and the young don't care or care too much.
I'll include Marcion and Alba's poodle,
the eyes of Cavalcanti's donna
and Querétaro that reflects the rose.
I'll find at daybreak cobwebs at the window
and at noon green grapes, metal lodes, cicada songs.
I'll calibrate the cost of boredom.

Sitting outside with loose papers on my lap,
a gust of wind blew the first best poem away.
It contained the usual clouds, love, Broadway
tunes, Mistral's tragic jackal. the river's bore.
I tracked it down the sandy paths
and through the thickets into cities, around corners
chasing cries of minds broken by the times.

This time I'll celebrate the thistles growing in the ditch,
embrace wife's winter, the shock of morning blue
in June, friendships, pratfalls, our echoes when we
finish shouting in the quarry, for this one will be, truly,
my best last effort.

Best Poem Ever 2

> I would like my last poem thus
> That it be gentle saying the simplest and least intended
> things

That it be ardent like a tearless sob
That it have the beauty of almost scentless flowers
The purity of the flame in which the most limpid diamonds
are consumed, the passion of suicides
who kill themselves without explanation.

   Manuel Bandeira, translated by Eliz. Bishop

Wind is swaying in the branches
and the voice of the telegraph is rising.
Bright patches of snow are all that's left
of my notebook. Sky, am I dreaming
or going completely blind?
And the day burning up like a blank page,
a little smoke and a little ash.
Do I know why I weep?
Singing and dying is all we can do.

     Mandelstam

Mandelstam Young & Old

Do I know why I weep?
Singing and dying is all we can do.
                    Mandelstam

Ars longa, vita brevis

www.ingramcontent.com/pod-product-compliance
Lightning Source LLC
Chambersburg PA
CBHW071459040426
42444CB00008B/1414